What Do
EXISTENTIALISTS
Believe?

Richard Appignanesi

Granta Books
London

Granta Publications, 2/3 Hanover Yard, Noel Road, London N1 8BE

First published in Great Britain by Granta Books 2006

A CIP catalogue record for this book is available
from the British Library.

ISBN-13: 978-1-86207-863-5
ISBN-10: 1-86207-863-7

1 3 5 7 9 10 8 6 4 2

Typeset by M Rules
Printed and bound in Great Britain by
Bookmarque Ltd, Croydon, Surrey

Contents

Introduction

What's in a name?

I do not like to talk about existentialism. It is the nature of an intellectual quest to be undefined. To name it and to define it is to wrap it up and tie the knot. What is left? A finished, already outdated mode of culture, something like a brand of soap – in other words, an idea.

Jean-Paul Sartre[1]

Existentialism is a seductive word. It promises to shed light on our human existence. I can assure the reader that existentialism does deliver rewarding insights. But not because existentialists speak with one consenting voice. Existentialists are not partners in a unified school of belief.

Existentialism is a recently invented term born in conflict. It was coined in 1944 by the French Catholic philosopher Gabriel Marcel (1889–1973). He sought to distance his own existential Catholicism from the atheist existentialism of Jean-Paul Sartre (1905–80).

Here are two initial existentialists already divided on the question of what to believe. The question is indeed vital but does not reduce existentialism to a quarrel between religious and irreligious strands of belief. The apparent disharmony between existentialists will be resolved in this book by asking two pertinent questions. What do existentialists believe *about themselves*? And what do existentialists *agree* on?

Existentialism is strangely nameless. A Christian is identified as a follower of Christ, a Marxist looks to Marx, a quantum physicist refers to quantum theory. Most systems have a party membership name. Existentialism is the dissident oddity without a figurehead or idea to authorize it but only the common situation of 'existence'.

What matters is not the name but the quest which motivates all existentialists. Their one common goal is to awaken our realization of *being in the world*. Existentialists ask us to linger meditatively on the sense of that word, *being*. What does it mean *to be*?

What does it mean to *be*?

I would say that everyone already is by necessity an existentialist. In the everyday, practical sense we are all existentialists, without knowing anything of some philosophy or other called existentialism. 'We get into the habit of living before acquiring the habit of thinking,' Albert Camus said.[2] He was speaking of the body's priority over mind in attaching us unquestioningly to life. *Being* is what concerns existentialists – the given situation that can never be taken for granted. The question of one's being must sooner or later come to mind, and when it does, one will instinctively think in an existentialist way. We naturally do so because existentialism does not demand conversion to some unknown faith. It is the recognition of the human viewpoint originally given to us.

Existentialists say we are 'thrown' into existence. It is easy to acknowledge what this means. We find ourselves conscious of being held in a situation which is limited to a specific time and space. Existence encounters itself as a fact that has already been determined without its consent. It might sometimes occur to me, in certain irksome moods, that I do not even exist as a truly 'consenting adult'. I feel opposed by a responsibility for *being* that I never asked for. Existence is some insulting joke played on me by I know not what – or more poignantly, *what for*. I sense my abandonment to a meaning which is not speaking any sense to me. I am in the dark of meaning.

Few of us have the leisure to contemplate the meaning of existence. We are preoccupied. Occupied means seized, taken possession of, by the tasks of everyday life. Honesty would require us to admit that the routine 'business of living' is not simply a constraint but a performance which serves to reward us with meaning and absolves us of having to think more than is called for. Common sense is able to 'take stock' – an apt business term – but regards thinking as an idle indulgence. Thinking is indeed against the grain of routine. But the word *pre*-occupied also means that routine goes far deeper than the employment we hope one day to retire from. It seeps into identity itself. I *am* the grocer, the stockbroker, the housewife, the football celebrity, a creature of ready-made institutional meaning. I cease to mean and become meant, very like an object is meant when I point to it.

The question of 'being meant' is a matter of fact from which we start. It is a fact that many of us are defined by a prior institutional belief, for instance, faith in some religion or faith in science. Or perhaps we don't know and are agnostic. Not to know is just as much a situation of belief as any traditional inheritance of faith, because these are existential facts, realities of *being* in the world.

The question existentialists address is this. What do I make of being *something* in the world? Is 'being Christian', for instance, really what I am? What is that question in actual fact, and in my actual circumstances, asking from me? It does not imply that existentialism wishes me to doubt my belief, or embrace some other belief or non-belief, but to face the consequences of *what I am being.*

Everyone is faced with the enigma of being in this world. '*I am*' can be declared in the fullness of joy. '*I am*' can also be the crushing burden of my depression. There are times when I can say 'things make sense', others when existence itself seems absurdly meaningless. These are not conditions that result primarily from thinking of them. They are experiences which come to us, so to speak, unthought of. Whatever sense an experience has can only come to me from being personally inside it.

What does it take to be an existentialist?

Existentialists have often been accused of taking interest only in the darkest, most negative emotions. Anxiety, despair, absurdity and suchlike are the supposed heraldry of existentialism. It has been belittled to a literature for pessimists. It can be asserted against this prejudice that, yes, existentialists are concerned with crisis, with life situations 'in the dark' of meaning, but only in order to reach a positive assertion of being. No religion or philosophy or science has ever begun by disguising the vicissitudes of existence. Darwin's picture of natural selection does not overwhelm us with optimism. Nor does Buddhism's view of suffering caused by human craving strike us as especially jovial.

What matters to existentialists is the dissidence by which human beings respond to a negative fate. I can illustrate this by a true account I heard some time ago on the radio.

The report tells of a man stranded on some barren peaks. I cannot recall if he suffered injury from a plane crash or mountaineering accident. Rescue was in any case far from sure. He had time enough to ponder his condition. What struck me was the revelation which came to him in his perilous isolation: *There is no God.* His certitude of a godless universe did not plunge him into despair, as might be supposed, but invigorated the conviction he needed to survive. Is it surprising that atheism can give reason to life?

We can imagine how similar circumstances could bring another person to the recognition of God's presence in the world and thereby sustain hope. Indeed, seclusion on remote mountains used to be the hermit's way of finding God. Our man on the mountain instead discovered no God.

The story suggests a point on which all existentialists agree: *meaning is inescapable.* This is not perhaps the reassurance we commonly expect from meaning. It is a disquieting meaning in which we seem imprisoned. But that is the point. The reassurance or disquiet I get from meaning will arise from the resolution of my being. Our man on the mountain found confident meaning in no God; another person might instead be driven by despair to sense God. This is not to say that meaning is 'relative' to their subjective situations. Meaning is in either case existentially full: there is no room for evasion. Meaning is inescapable precisely because it can never be relative. It is entirely what I find myself *being*.

I have declared my belief that we are all existentialists in practice. It is the task of this book to test that belief in a series of thought experiments linked by explanatory interludes. A story from life might help to clarify the existentialist practice adopted in this book.

Jean-Paul Sartre tells the story of a student who came to him with a dilemma. France at the time was occupied by Nazi Germany. The student's elder brother had been killed in the German offensive of 1940. His father was believed a collaborator. The young man burned to avenge his brother and rectify the shame of his father's treason. He entertained the risk of setting out for England to join the Free French Forces there. But he hesitated to do this. His mother lived alone with him and her one consolation was in this young man. His disappearance, and perhaps his death, would plunge her into despair. He had to choose between devotion to one individual or moral action for his country. What should he do?

Sartre answered him: 'You are free, therefore choose – that is to say, invent. No rule of general morality can show you what you ought to do: no signs are vouchsafed in this world.'

Sartre was later criticized for not being more helpful.

He replied: 'If someone comes to you for advice, it is because the answer has already been chosen.'[3]

Sartre does not propose a neat solution to the untidiness of life situations. His interest in this story is to stimulate a *thought experiment* on decision. Decision will often entail regret.

The choice of one possibility has the conclusive effect of amputating other ones. There is a further implied limitation on decision. The individual never figures alone in taking a decision but in awareness of a situation circumstantially affected by events beyond one's control. In the young man's case these are his brother's death, his father's alleged treason, his mother's affliction and of course the Nazi Occupation. We call this the unforeseen circumstances of history which seem to preordain our choices.

Sartre's anecdote signposts a route that we shall follow. The reader will encounter various existentialist thought experiments usually preceded by 'interludes' of miniature briefings on the historical situations which circumscribe those experiments.

First thought experiment

What are existentialist questions?

Belief is never the answer but always the problem.
Existentialist questions are posed in the light of this fundamental principle; answers which presume a given belief are not valid for existentialists.

Suppose I am minded to ask, 'Why should I be at all?' The question might be asked in curiosity or bewilderment, in exasperation or even in utter boredom with life. It does not seem to presume a belief but rather a lack of one. I appear to be asking what philosophers call the basic ontological question of what being *is*. But to ask 'why' I exist exceeds the limits of the fact that I have existence. I want to know more than the mere fact that *I am*. I do not linger on the sense itself of 'being', as existentialists ask me to do, but hanker after the 'why' of it.

I cannot for long sustain my concentration simply on being without wandering off to ready-made cosmic answers. I will be tempted to find a religious solution in 'God's creation' or, if I am scientifically minded, in a randomly spawned universe. Ingenious beliefs of all sorts will occur to distract me, everything except to stay fixed on the *be* in 'Why should I *be* at all?'

Existentialists say I am avoiding the responsibility I bear of being *present* in this world.

Suppose I ask the common-sense question, 'What should I believe?' To which domains of belief should I address myself? Should I turn to religion or science for my answer? I may indeed end up satisfied – or not – with a belief. But I am not answered. Existentialists say that I am always left to account for *being*. Something remains left over that cannot ever be classified. Let us call it a margin of freedom of which I am conscious, particularly when I ask myself the unwelcome existential question, 'Is *what I am* really a matter of my own choice?' This is an instance of *being* in disquiet.

Suppose, in my disquiet, I am led to religion for an answer. If so, I will then find myself questioned, 'What does faith ask of me?' That question is always up to date, it concerns me in the present, but it also carries an immense burden of history. What faith asks of me now is something that links me to its origin in the past – to the teachings of Christ or Buddha or the Prophet Muhammad or other traditions. I can seek in the present to recover the pristine purity of a faith 'in its origin', so to speak, as some fundamentalist Christians or Islamists do. But I am left to decide what to do about the rival presence of science and technology which claim that verifiable information has replaced faith.

The basic *existential* question remains unanswered by belief. My existence is itself in question. 'Being in question' will inevitably raise questions of freedom, consciousness, moral value, action, and the significance of history. But these questions are the very ones which underpin the designated beliefs of theology, philosophy, science, psychology, ethics and all other systems. Existentialists begin from the unresolved questions on which systems attempt to build impersonal beliefs.

The existentialist way of questioning will become clearer as we proceed.

Interlude

How did existentialism start?

Existentialism coincides with the advance of a modern scientific world view. It is a response specific to the emergence of science which places religion on the defensive. We are looking back to the European foundations of science in the seventeenth century when the question of 'what is true to belief' passes to the entirely new status of 'what is objectively valid'. Truth is that which can be experimentally verified. Human consciousness itself becomes an object of scientific inquiry. Thinking is submitted for the first time to the test of rigorous measurement. Is the mind capable of being *undeceived* in its comprehension of reality? Science originates by asking how reliable the mind is. History turns at this moment to free-thinking.

Free-thinking modern philosophy begins with the French mathematician René Descartes (1596–1650). His well-known maxim 'I think therefore I am' underpins an edifice of rational scepticism on this simple premise: 'The one thing that cannot be doubted is doubt itself.' It is an agenda for the empirical pursuit of evidence. The search for the indubitable – that which cannot be further reduced to doubt – must begin from doubting everything.

Existentialism enters on stage when the drama of meaningful existence becomes a contest between free-thinking doubt and belief.

René Descartes viewed consciousness as a substance distinct from the body. The body is a non-conscious machine common to all animals. His conviction led him to suppose that the cries of a vivisected animal were simply the noises of a machine being disassembled.

Second thought experiment

Pascal's wager

. . . let us act as if we had only eight hours to live.

Blaise Pascal[4]

What do you make of this argument for religious belief?

Either God is or is not. Which side shall we take? Reason can decide nothing here. For, if God does exist, we are grappling with an infinitely incomprehensible being, without limits, who bears no relation to our finite limits of reason. Does such a Supreme Being exist? Your choice is down to the fall of a coin, either heads or tails, yes or no. On which will you gamble? To accept belief in God, and live by the teachings of faith, is the wisest bet. If the bet is won, you gain the rewards of eternity. If the bet is lost, you forfeit some insignificant pleasures. The alternative of unbelief at best enjoys those short-lived earthly pleasures, but at worst incurs eternal loss.

Does it convince you to gamble on belief?

This is the 'wager' famously proposed by Blaise Pascal (1623–62). Pascal was a French scientific genius celebrated for his experimental proof of the vacuum, his work on the mathematics of the cycloid, the geometry of conic sections and the arithmetic triangle. He was also a practical inventor who gave us the calculating machine, the first public bus service, the first syringe and first wristwatch.

The most relevant objection to Pascal's wager is an existential one. I cannot simply decide to make myself believe in something, however advisable it might seem. Pascal's reply to that is also existential. Faith can only have the opportunity of proving itself on me if I live as if it were true. I can change my mode of behaviour, subdue my passions, pray, attend church, and so on, in the effort to nourish my belief. Do not most believers in God already live like this in the exercise of their faith? This is psychologically true but existentially limited. His argument hinges on the doctrine of Christian faith which presupposes God. What sense would that make to a Hindu or Buddhist?

But that is not the concern of Pascal's wager. He is addressing the post-Christian free-thinker whose contemplation of eternity does not kindle the least spark of faith. Pascal understood as a scientist that no amount of thought can suffice for a *convincing* faith. He himself had explicitly formulated a method of proof by mathematical induction. But something else is necessary – a probability beyond the limits of reason. His wager is a last-ditch attempt at 'artificial respiration of the soul' for those unsure of having one. What more was Pascal seeking?

The idea of a calculating machine came to Pascal at the age of nineteen. He spent five years detailing its construction to unskilled workmen. The effort aggravated the severity of his chronic headaches and weakened his health. The machines, manufactured and finally placed on sale in 1652, earned him a trifling sum.

What should I believe?

> For after all, what is man in nature? A nothing in compari-
> son with the infinite, an absolute in comparison with
> nothing, a central point between nothing and all. Infinitely
> far from understanding these extremes, the end of things
> and their beginning are hopelessly hidden from him in an
> impenetrable secret. He is equally capable of seeing the noth-
> ingness from which he came and the infinite in which he is
> engulfed.
>
> *Blaise Pascal* [5]
>
> I believe; Lord, help my unbelief!
>
> *Mark 9:23*

Pascal is the first to express a modern existential anguish which
comes from having to choose between the imperatives of science and religion. Miguel de Unamuno, the Spanish Catholic
existentialist, said in 1923 that reading Pascal's book of *Pensées*
was to 'enter into the sanctuary of a naked soul' and see the
heart wrestling with an obstinate head. [6] A head afflicted all of
his life by ferocious headaches, due to a congenital malforma-
tion of the skull, until his death at thirty-nine. Pascal's head
suffered too from the grave ills of his time. He grew up in a
Europe plunged for almost a century in destructive religious
wars. Catholic and Protestant disputants alike had lost credi-
bility in the eyes of a new class of 'libertines', scientific and
materialist-minded free-thinkers, agnostics if not outright athe-
ists. A new age of rational progress known as the Enlightenment
had begun to dawn in the midst of Europe's slaughterhouse, in
a world of collapsed values and moral decadence. Pascal is our
contemporary, familiar to us, in Hannah Arendt's words, as a
'man in dark times'.

Pascal's head inclined to free-thinking science but his heart was drawn to the 'moral vacuum'. He committed himself to the outspoken defence of Jansenism, a form of Catholic Puritanism, in his *Lettres provinciales* of 1656–7. Jansenism upholds the belief that salvation can only be had by the gift of grace and not by man's will which is hopelessly deficient. This essentially Protestant idea was condemned by the Catholic Church and bitterly contested by the Jesuits.

Why did Pascal choose to sustain an extreme fundamentalist faith which put him at risk of persecution from the Catholic authorities? Why not a more moderate belief in tune with reason? It was a possibility available to him in two forms. The Catholic Church in this period of acute moral exhaustion had its own religious libertines, the Jesuits, able power-brokers and theologians of compromise. The Jesuits offered *probabilism* as a flexible solution to ethics. Probabilism states that in cases of insoluble doubt concerning the moral legitimacy of an act, it is permissible to perform the act if sound reasons can be adduced in its favour, regardless of whether the opposite opinion can be sustained with equally valid reasons. What else is Pascal's wager but a probabilist argument? True, but ethics is not religion. Pascal's concern is with faith in the hidden recesses of the heart. That is why he cannot permit himself the second way out. He could have opted as many libertines did to place faith outside the bounds of reason. This was Descartes's own Jesuitical concession to religion which Pascal deplores. 'I cannot forgive Descartes. He would gladly have left God out of his whole philosophy. But he could not help making Him give one last flip to set the world in motion. After that he had no more use for God.'[7]

Pascal will not settle for a faith 'out of bounds' of reason. It is the scientist in him who wishes after the impossible. He comes to the desperate point of willingness even to sacrifice science. 'I agree that Copernicus' theories can be left unexamined. But this! It is a matter of life and death to know whether the soul is mortal or immortal.'[8]

Albert Camus, an atheist existentialist, will echo this thought three hundred years later. 'Whether the earth or the sun revolves around the other is a matter of profound indifference. To tell the truth, it is a futile question. On the other hand, I see many people die because they judge that life is not worth living.'[9]

Pascal, like Camus, is troubled by 'what it means to be'. But unlike Camus he does not think the cosmology of Galileo and Copernicus is futile. Far worse, to his mind, it has opened up a speculative void not only 'out there' in space but within human thought. 'The eternal silence of those infinite spaces strikes me with terror.'[10] A thrilling prospect of space travel was already envisioned in the science fiction of Pascal's day. That is not what he dreads. He says elsewhere: 'It is not in space that I must seek my dignity, but by the control of my thoughts. [. . .] In space the Universe encompasses me and swallows me like a dot; in thought I encompass the Universe.'[11] What strikes him with terror is the 'eternal silence' of his own thought encompassing nothing. Pascal had experimented scientifically on the vacuum and now found 'proof of the void' within himself. Jean-Paul Sartre would survey that inner void in his treatise *Being and Nothingness* in the twentieth century.

Pascal is the first existentialist to identify a 'God-shaped hole' in human existence. He foresaw that the crisis of belief would from now on be permanent. Not only faith but *being religious* had been called into question. Religious experience could not offer reason for its validity. Pascal gave stark expression to what philosophers call *fideism,* the conviction that faith surpasses rational standards. To put it another way: belief in faith itself is the only grounds for belief.

Interlude

Kierkegaard: The Age of Anxiety

> The human heart has a tiresome tendency to label as fate only what crushes it. But happiness likewise, in its way, is without reason, since it is inevitable. Modern man, however, takes the credit for it himself, when he doesn't fail to recognize it.
>
> *Albert Camus* [12]

Pascal had stumbled on the fundamental existentialist principle: belief is never the answer but always the problem. Evidently so, because believing in something is the existential issue facing us all, and belief is liable to deception. We all seek to be *undeceived* believers in what makes sense for us. Precisely this contradiction at the heart of 'undeceived belief' concerns all existentialists, religious or not.

The Danish philosopher Søren Kierkegaard (1813–55) is usually named the founder of existentialism. He follows after the French Revolution which had deified Supreme Reason, elevated the guillotine and ended in the battlefield carnage of the Napoleonic era. Europe since Pascal carried on being an accommodating cemetery of disillusioned hopes and ideas. But it manifested one last titanic idol of Reason in the idealist philosophy of Kierkegaard's predecessor, the German philosopher G. W. F. Hegel (1770–1831). It is well to remember that Kierkegaard and Karl Marx were contemporaries and that both rejected their spiritual father Hegel – but that no word on politics ever crossed Kierkegaard's lips.

Kierkegaard enters the stage at a moment of restored conservatism in Europe. Copenhagen offered him security and no apparent reason for complaint. True, he suffered a slight curvature of the spine and frail health, but was otherwise privileged. A fortune inherited at his father's death in 1838 gave him the leisure to spend a lifetime writing books of spectacular dissidence. He came to upset the tranquillity of his home town by revolutionizing the sense of everyday existence. Kierkegaard identified what we now call 'the Age of Anxiety'.

Kierkegaard exposed the 'dread' hidden under the safe conduct of normality. Dread seeps into one's life from the anxiety that can sometimes overwhelm and paralyse the self. It might arise from sensing oneself alone in the cosmos but does not require even this specific thought. His concept of dread speaks to us of moments in which the self experiences a threat of collapse. I might suddenly feel an absence of whatever it is that I take for granted to maintain my capabilities. My intentions, my will, my ego are at a loss to make sense of existence. I am faced with my own possible nonbeing. Such instances of dread are useful in Kierkegaard's view to unmask what is false in my normal determinations of who I am. The process of 'who I am' is interrupted in its continuity by the suddenness and urgency of anxiety. Time itself is disrupted by a disorientating anxiety which is present at one moment, and gone the next, but only to become totally and completely present again. It does not fit our expectations but tortures them with uncertainty.

Anxiety unravels the inadequacies and self-deceptions of what we *think* we believe.

Do not get the impression of a gloomy Dane. You will find exuberant wit and a passion for life in his writings. Kierkegaard takes his seriousness lightly and often mocks himself. He seldom published in his own name but adopted extravagantly comic pseudonyms suited to particular works: Johannes de Silentio, Anti-Climacus, Vigilius Haufniensis and many others.

There was a purpose in this. He intended us to see that ideas do not benefit from any authority. The author is himself a sort of fiction whose thoughts are presented as different modes of being for the reader's own judgement and choice. Kierkegaard is modern, if not postmodern, in declaring that philosophy is nothing more than a practice of writing akin to autobiography or novels. Existentialists of every colour are indebted to him for placing the actual conditions of existence before philosophy's abstract concepts. Being precedes thinking. This is a reversal of Descartes's maxim, 'I think therefore I am.' Existentialists after Kierkegaard say instead, 'I am conditionally *this* being which thinks.'

Third thought experiment

The absurdity of faith

'The great earthquake', as Kierkegaard called it, occurred in 1835 when his father confessed a terrible secret. His father, Michael Kierkegaard, began life miserably poor in rural Jutland. He was sent by chance to an uncle in Copenhagen, a trader in woollens, and thereafter his luck changed and he prospered. His several properties escaped destruction during the British bombardment of 1807; he was one of the few not ruined by the state bankruptcy of 1813. He seemed miraculously fortunate. Michael was a strict Lutheran, an overpowering and imaginative personality, fond of logical argument. But a sense of disquiet underlay his piety. He revealed why to his son.

One day, in Michael's hungry boyhood, enraged by divine indifference to his sufferings, he had stood on a hill and solemnly cursed God. He became convinced of God's punishment when death arrived in the midst of good fortune to strike down his family. It was indeed true, for Kierkegaard had seen his mother and five of his six brothers and sisters die, one after the other. He too now became haunted by his father's certainty of God's retribution. He threw himself at this point into a 'life of dissipation', which he probably exaggerated for the benefit of his fiancée Regine Olsen.

Kierkegaard fell in love with eighteen-year-old Regine and became engaged to her in 1840. He was twenty-five, wealthy, and recently graduated with a Master's degree in theology; and she, intelligent and attractive, would have made a 'respectable match'. He broke off the engagement a year later. The reason given to her was the guilt burdening him from his days of student debauchery – much as he later portrayed the 'seducer' in his book *Either/Or* – but he acknowledged in himself a melancholic complexity which opened another gulf between them. He posed as a 'corrupt scoundrel' to disillusion her. Better a deception than expose Regine to his life of predestined suffering which he felt was his certain heritage. He tested the limits of ethics by sacrificing love and respectability to an uncommon ideal of faith. It was a faith which responded existentially to the 'absurdity' of his father's dread of God.

Michael Kierkegaard mirrors a type of Job figure whose faith is sorely tested by a whimsical God. Kierkegaard transmuted Michael's story into that of another Biblical patriarch, Abraham, for his book *Fear and Trembling*, published soon after his break with Regine. Abraham in old age had been miraculously blessed with a son, Isaac, and was then commanded by God to sacrifice him as a proof of faith. Abraham was prepared to obey. Isaac was spared death at the last instant by the intervention of an angel.

... when I have to think of Abraham, I am as though annihilated. I catch sight every moment of that enormous paradox which is the substance of Abraham's life, every moment I am repelled, and my thought in spite of all its passion cannot get a hair's breadth further. I strain every muscle to get a view of it – that very instant I am paralysed.

It is a dreadful story. Can we believe in a repellently cruel God who tempts a father to butcher and burn his son? The literal truth of the story is not the point of Kierkegaard's psychological analysis. He asks us to consider what is indeed possibly a supreme fiction of pure faith. It has everything to do with deception. Would you not, in Abraham's place, begin to doubt your own sanity? Would you not question a command that makes absolutely no sense? Would you not think yourself deceived by a 'voice' tempting you commit a sinful atrocity? What assurance do you have of being justified in your act? There is none. Abraham faces the quicksand of abysmal dread. He is Kierkegaard's 'Knight of Faith'.

Kierkegaard is in fact testing the Lutheran doctrine of salvation by justification of faith alone. Martin Luther's teaching was that Christ's death on the cross had paid the entire debt of all our sins forever. It leaves us with the only assurance we have of being saved. I cannot personally atone for my sins because that work of redeeming has already been done by Christ's suffering. All I can do is willingly accept the Saviour who justifies my faith.

Faith is born from the self's despair that it can ever do anything for its own salvation. One must truly despair, truly 'come to nothing', before turning the corner and surrendering oneself to the inward relief of faith. Faith demands genuine indifference to what will become of one. 'It is taken care of; now, be at peace.'

There is a kernel of existential truth in Luther's insight. Kierkegaard is aware of it but not assured by despairing passivity. Despair is for him a 'sickness unto death', a mortal offence against the freedom of the spirit. One does not 'give up' to faith; one does not 'fall' into it, as if into sleep. It is instead the resolution of a fully conscious choice which requires one to 'leap into faith', as Kierkegaard says. Faith is an absurdity. Or, as he also puts it, an 'objective uncertainty'.

Something else is clear to Kierkegaard. Lutheran faith rests on an intellectually constructed notion of unearned grace which denies free will. It presumes the *idea* of a once-and-for-all redemption. This is not an existentially genuine faith. Kierkegaard deliberately chooses Abraham for his 'Knight of Faith', who comes before any glimmer of the redeeming Christ, as if to underline the existentialist credo that 'being precedes thinking'. I exist without reassurance of thinking. How can I be assured that what I do, what I believe in or even disbelieve, is justified? It is an impossible demand. To *be* assured – which means to *exist* in assurance – is an existential fiction. More precisely, it is self-deception, or bad faith.

Kierkegaard's existentialist teaching

Søren Kierkegaard presented an odd figure in the streets of Copenhagen. Cartoons of the time pilloried his stove-pipe hat, narrow trousers, perennial umbrella and stooped walk. He repaid the unkindness with his own wry humour. 'It is my fate to be trampled to death by geese.' We might wonder if this irony is directed against himself or the good citizens who mocked him.

Luther's reformed Protestant theology was the foundation of the Established Church of Denmark. It was to these 'righteously justified' Christians of his day that Kierkegaard addressed his paradox of absurd faith. He felt increasingly obliged to attack the scandal of 'Christendom', his term of sarcasm for a public of superficially conformist Christians shepherded by a clergy become mere state civil servants. Faith had been betrayed to Christendom's guise of respectability. Kierkegaard's task was to discomfit the complacent by reminding them of faith's existential basis.

But that's just it. There is no reasonable basis for faith. Faith is absurd. The existence of God and all related ethical claims are 'objective uncertainties' for which there can be no adequate proof. Faith is in this sense baseless, a chasm, a leap into the unknown. 'The Voice' which Abraham heeds can only be his own, in strict terms of undeceived reality. It can only be our resolution too, in undeceived reality, which takes heed of choice and performs accordingly. Kierkegaard asks to us consider this carefully. 'Whose voice is it that calls on me to be undeceived by my own doings?' Is it conscience? Or is conscience an alibi which bad faith gives to disguise our fear of inescapable meaning?

The early Church Father Tertullian (c.160–c.220) had said, *Credo quia absurdum*: 'I believe because it is absurd.' Luther's case rests on this progression of faith. Kierkegaard is saying something quite different – *belief* is itself absurd. Belief, not believing in something, is our existential problem. Kierkegaard does allow for true or false propositions, accessible to practical test, and upon which I am permitted to say 'I believe this to be true' or not. He does not disclaim reason but asks the question scientifically relevant to us, 'What do you believe *belief* is?' 'Evidence' is the obvious answer of reason; but evidence is not a matter of faith. A chasm of absurdity gapes between belief – in the ordinary sense of what I think it is – and belief which is called to risk.

The absurd normally means for us the senseless. But for Kierkegaard it has a distinct function which refers to the original Latin root of (ab)*surdus* (deaf, mute, silent), understood as the 'unheard of'. So that when Kierkegaard says we exist 'in the power of the absurd', he means 'in the power of the unheard of'. He intends a commanding silence that arises from our own overwhelmed realization of being thrown into the world. The absurd is in this sense a *summons*, an insistence for answer that the world voices in us. Kierkegaard looks beyond conscience to a radical consciousness of being which risks being unheard of. Existentialists will thereafter follow Kierkegaard in building on this meaning of the absurd.

Philosophy is there in our everyday language which has grown stale from habit. The very words that we most commonly use – choice, possibility, decision, action and others of daily coin – are in need of existentialist rescue. What has 'choice' become for us today? Little more than a logo of consumerism. And what of 'decision'? It has been usurped by the agendas of corporate management and political spin doctors. The more problematic Big Words – freedom, value, humanity, reality – have become even fuzzier to our ears. Existentialism restores such words to their original summons of meaning – to the absurd, in Kierkegaard's sense of being 'unheard of'.

Kierkegaard's hardest thought

The absurd has another application. Kierkegaard identified an irreducible absurdity in the modern pursuit of certainty. Reason cannot resolve the unknown, he tells us. Why is that? Because for reason to do this, it would have to recognize itself in the unknown which is its absolute unlikeness, and reason cannot do this without risk of negating itself. Kierkegaard puts it thus: 'reason conceives only of such an unknown within itself that it

can conceive by means of itself'.[13] Reason, by its own definition, can only ever be reasonable to *itself.* Reason cannot
'transcend itself' to conceive of a superiority outside its own
means. The unknown is reason's own inaccessible exteriority,
the absurd, at which it must stop short.

But reason is also the lee-side of the unknown that allows for
our freedom of choice. Faith is the choice one has of abandon-
ing the shelter of reason and leaping, in full awareness, into the
unknown. This is Abraham's drama which Kierkegaard attends
in 'fear and trembling'. No certainty is ever possible. If one's
belief is genuine, and not a sham of bad faith, it will always have
the consequence of troubling one's existence. Kierkegaard tells
us, 'only one deception is possible in the infinite sense – self-
deception'.[14] What does he mean by 'infinite'? Is it the same
limit of certainty that tortured Pascal?

Interlude

Nietzsche: The Darwinian Age

Kierkegaard's attack on Christendom settled accounts both with his father's guilt-ridden piety and Denmark's shallow Christian respectability. The German philosopher Friedrich Nietzsche (1844–1900) went further in his atheistic attack on the entire system of Christian values that supported Western civilization.

There are features of similarity between them. Nietzsche's father had been a Lutheran pastor in a line of clergymen. Nietzsche studied theology at university, together with classical philology, and was expected to follow in the clerical tradition. His health was poor and, also like Kierkegaard's, his writings show a remarkable heterogeneity of styles, a play of contrary voices more poetic in character than technically philosophic.

Nietzsche's difference from Kierkegaard is not simply one of atheism but of prophesying a darker age in gestation. For one thing, Nietzsche is witness to the formation of an imperially aggressive Germany. His health first became compromised in 1867 while serving in the Prussian army and was permanently ruined during volunteer service as a medical orderly in the Franco-Prussian War of 1870. His collapse into insanity for the last decade of his life seems due to syphilis contracted during his military episodes. He died at the threshold of the twentieth century, in 1900, and his sister Elisabeth gained control over his literary estate. Elisabeth Förster, the widow of a notorious ultra-nationalist anti-Semite, misused her executory power to recreate an image of Nietzsche that would accord with her final years of enthusiasm for Adolf Hitler. Nietzsche, the prescient foe of 'bestial anti-Semitism', 'German stupidity' and its 'barbaric nationalism', ended up as a standard issue textbook in the rucksacks of German soldiers in both World Wars.

Nietzsche stands as gateway witness to other twentieth-century turmoils. Militarist nationalism grew in deadlock with socialist internationalism, as he could see in Bismarck's struggles against Germany's steadily advancing Marxist workers' party. Industrial technology, capitalist imperialism and mass revolution appeared the unstoppable engines of progress. Nietzsche's insights are shaped by a Darwinian age in which force declares itself a scientific question. What sort of existence will the future prove best fitted to survive and conquer?

Nietzsche's brilliance as a classical scholar earned him a professorship at twenty-five without completing the normally stipulated doctoral thesis. He laboured unhappily for ten years in the philologist's 'mole-like activities', as he wryly commented, before his deteriorating health caused him to resign his professorial chair at the University of Basel in 1879. He had ten more years left to produce books that hardly anyone read, in conditions of infirmity, semi-blindness and minimal human contact as he wandered the boarding-houses of Europe.

Fourth thought experiment

Beyond good and evil

> A revaluation of all values, this question-mark so black, so huge it casts a shadow over him who sets it up – such a destiny of a task compels one every instant to run out into the sunshine so as to shake off a seriousness grown all too oppressive.
>
> *Nietzsche*[15]

Nietzsche undertook the mission of 'revaluating all values' as one might seek to breathe clean mountain air. His own ill health drove him to seek health for others. Nietzsche's mission can be encapsulated in a single therapeutic aim: how does one exist in ethically sound health?

Nietzsche begins from a radically simple observation. Life does not in itself possess intrinsic factual value. It only has the value we assign to it. What is also strikingly evident is that human existence has never ceased being evaluated. It has always been assumed to require *explanation*. The first question to ask is not why life should need answering but what the answers say about the health of those who believe them true. Evaluations can therefore be decoded as symptoms of the condition of the evaluator. The prescriber is unmasked by his prescription. This amounts to a therapeutic *undoing* of all the therapies that have hitherto prescribed explanatory 'meanings' to human life. Is life truly a sickness in need of remedy? Might it be that the sickness belongs to the evaluators who urge upon us their anti-dotes to life? Suppose, on the basis of this question, we probe the given values of Western philosophy, religion and morality. What fundamental expressions of health or sickness might we uncover?

Nietzsche recommends starting with the human experience of suffering. What do we gain from experiencing it? What indeed, if religion had not come to prize it. Christianity has done wonders for suffering by conceptualizing its opposite in a promise of eter-nal release from pain in this life. It has immortalized suffering by endowing it with ultimate significance in the hereafter. Suffering gains from the immense flattery of a cosmic reason, and is thereby tranquillized. Reality gets twisted round to yield a 'truer' reality elsewhere which is settled by the value of suffering in this one. It would seem in the end better to suffer than not to.

We live in order to be saved from life. This is the explanation for existence given by what Nietzsche calls the 'ascetic ideal'. Asceticism privileges suffering as a means to achieve the insight of renunciation which alone can grant our salvation from this world of illusions. The ascetic ideal underpins all religions but is especially interesting in Western Christian civilization because it has cunningly survived a transformation into secular exis-tence. We might think this rather odd. Can it be that scientific materialism has not done away with the Christian fantasy of immortality? Has not secular common sense discarded the Christian renunciation of this world? Are we not realists offended by suffering – who seek practical measures to rid our-selves of it? Surely this must be as plain as the nose on Nietzsche's face?

Nietzsche famously said that he 'philosophizes with a hammer' – not brutally, as this is often taken to mean, but delicately, 'as with a tuning fork', the light tap that makes audible the hollowness of idols. The idols that he sounds out for answer are the eternal ones, 'none more hollow' yet 'most believed in', which occupy the present market place.[16] Nietzsche seeks 'beyond good and evil' for what he calls the 'genealogy of morals'. Genealogy indicates that values have a human ancestry and not any divine or transcendental provenance. They are, in one of his favourite words, 'timely', or seasonable, implying that they are liable to decay and become untimely if they exceed their span. Western values are in this sense the untimely vestiges of a decadence that has long outlived itself. Christianity supplied the 'idol' which decadent Western societies go on worshipping in twilight shapes no longer resembling their origin. But genealogy can trace them back to their Christian fabrication.

'Denial of life' is the hollow sound we must listen for, under Nietzsche's hammer. And what do we hear of it today? It is now believed good to prolong youthfulness. Enhancements of all kinds, and not only the extreme of cosmetic surgery, are on offer to service a worry generally experienced by Westerners. Does it not sound like a fear that cannot bear reminders of life's traces – that wishes for a 'beyond the here and now' of mortal flesh, that craves for *untimeliness*? Have we truly renounced immortality or gone further to materialize it? Part-replacement surgery is but a timid step in the direction of genetic manipulation which aims in the future to eliminate death. 'The last enemy that shall be destroyed is death,' St Paul vowed in Corinthians I, 26. Christianity wished a finite life resurrected to infinity. Ours is instead a twilight Christianity of modern Egyptian immortalists who wish to embalm themselves genetically.

Let us be clear. The question of immortality's material possibility takes its answer in the *spirit* of the wish. It is begotten by something *wanting* in us.

I have thrown Nietzsche forward to post-Christian secular conditions. He would not be surprised by our material commitment to salvation from life. All of Western philosophy has been steadily declining towards that goal of 'denial of life' ever since Plato began teaching a higher spiritual truth. Christianity empowered the idea of absolute truth by wedding it to the ascetic ideal of 'slave morality'.

What does Nietzsche mean by slave morality? 'Good' and 'bad' were originally non-moral descriptions of character. The warrior of ancient times favoured the attributes of pride, autonomy and competition. Christianity converted these virtues of mastery into vices. Pride becomes a grave sin, competition surrenders to charity, autonomy kneels in obedience. The weak take 'slave morality' vengeance on the strong and triumph as 'the meek who shall inherit the earth'. Good and evil are thereafter 'facts of conscience' measured by inscrutable divine authority. Introspection comes into being for the first time and is at once exposed to the vagaries of bad faith.

Nietzsche, in his twilight years, became addicted to some mysterious Javanese drug – possibly opium – taken to relieve his acute pain and insomnia. The Genealogy of Morals, completed in just fifteen days in 1887, was written in this sadly debilitated condition. Two years later, in Turin, he saw a coachman whipping an old horse. He embraced the animal's neck, sobbed, and fainted away into a permanent state of insanity.

Is God dead?

Nietzsche gives another name to bad faith or self-deception. He calls it *nihilism*. Taken from the Latin *nihil*, 'nothing', it literally means nothing-ism or belief in nothing. Nietzsche's sense of it refers to the an*nihil*ation of values consequent upon the ascetic ideal. It does not mean believing in nothing, but worse, believing in values harmful to the human species. The last sentence of Nietzsche's *Genealogy of Morals* declares: 'Man would sooner have the void for his purpose than be void of purpose.' This is the summation of nihilistic value.

Nietzsche believed himself untimely. He had come too early for a proper hearing in his own age of 'passive nihilism', a time not yet aware that the foundations of morality had subsided into a decadence in which existence would finally be found purposeless and meaningless. The advent is strikingly told: 'God is dead.' Nietzsche puts this news into the mouth of a madman who carries a lantern in broad daylight as he searches everywhere for the vanished God.

To say that God is 'dead' implies that there once was a living God. It is not a statement of atheistic denial but the diagnosis of a condition. 'God's death' opens a void in place of that which hitherto gave the resonant sound of value to all actions. Value has itself 'gone dead'.

God's death, in Nietzsche's sense, is to see that void in the full glare of noonday. It presents us with a freedom devoid of *any* explanation – a value*less* freedom beyond good and evil, and hence beyond choice. It is our 'condemnation to freedom', as Sartre will later say. Nietzsche predicts that modern nihilism, in semi-conscious dread of such freedom, would pass at once to new idols of self-deception. The nation-state, liberal democracy and socialism must each proceed scientifically and in the name of universal brotherhood to annihilate the earth. Nietzsche's modern gospel – the glad tidings of God's death – is intentionally ironic. He speaks of a future already taken place.

Who is Nietzsche's listener? This is another way of asking: who is the object of history? Nietzsche believed that every individual exists in unresolved tension between the characteristic 'master-and-slave' traits. We are existentially trapped in *perspectivism* which holds that there are no moral facts but only interpretations of them. There is no escaping the restrictions on our knowledge that impose a limited perspective on what we choose to value. No 'God's-eye prospect' of the world can be assumed. It is in this very struggle between competing values to achieve the ultimate 'good' that Nietzsche discovers the instinctual 'will to power'. He does not intend a brute 'wilfulness to power', agreeable to Nazis, but growth that seeks to endure. It is opposed by the values symptomatic of decline, the nihilistic ones, which Sigmund Freud would later controversially name the 'death instinct'.

How can we be assured that our sense of value does not mask a deficient health? Nietzsche asks us to consider the Christian ascetic ideal: 'Do unto others as you would have them do unto you.' This is an ethic motivated by fear of retaliation. It advises me to curb my actions on the possibility that others might reply in kind. Restraint by timidity can only lead to resentment concealed in bad faith. The great eighteenth-century Enlightenment philosopher Immanuel Kant reformulated this Christian moral principle into what he called the Categorical Imperative: 'Always act so that you are able to will that the maxim of your action should also be a universal law of nature.' Nietzsche wonders what sort of impersonal maxim of action could possibly authorize a 'universal law of nature'. Is this not to outfit the ascetic ideal in the Emperor's new clothes? A case, once again, of encouraging bad faith?

Nietzsche rebels against all ethical doctrines in which deceit lurks under the guise of selflessness. He proposes instead a Yea-saying affirmation of life, a will to 'eternal recurrence'. Eternal recurrence is posed as a question: 'How well disposed would a person have to become to himself and to life to crave nothing more fervently than the infinite repetition, without alteration, of each and every moment?' The idea came to Nietzsche one day in 1881 whilst on a walk in Sils Maria, Switzerland.[17] I can compare this to Kierkegaard's concept of repetition:

> Repetition and recollection are the same movement, only in opposite directions; for what is recollected has been, is repeated backwards, whereas repetition properly so called is recollected forwards. Therefore repetition, if it is possible, makes a man happy, whereas recollection makes him unhappy . . .[18]

The point is that anyone who could joyfully embrace the repetition of an entire life – without self-deception or 'editing out' a single of its unpleasant aspects or horrors – would be a super-human being. Nietzsche gives the name *Übermensch* ('super' or 'over'- man) to this creature of superlative self-mastery 'whose distance from the ordinary man is greater than the distance between man and ape'. Such a person comes into being by answering 'yes' to Nietzsche's question: 'Can I bear the unsparing light of eternal recurrence?'

Interlude

How existentialism can go wrong

> Islam is not a heritage of any particular race or country; this is
> God's religion and it is for the whole world. It has the right to
> destroy all obstacles in the form of institutions and traditions
> which limit man's freedom of choice. It does not attack indi-
> viduals nor does it force them to accept its beliefs; it attacks
> institutions and traditions to release human beings from their
> poisonous influences which distort human nature and which
> curtail human freedom.
>
> *Sayyid Qutb*[19]

Sayyid Qutb (1906–66) is the main ideologist of modern
Muslim Sunni fundamentalism. This frail scholarly Egyptian
inspired a creed which led directly to the Islamist terrorism of
Al-Qaeda and the catastrophe of September 11th.

Qutb was not an ignorant fanatic but well-versed in Western
literature, philosophy and science. He spent twenty-one months
in 1949–50 visiting universities in the United States on a
research mission for the Egyptian Ministry of Education. He
became embroiled in alleged conspiracies to overthrow Egypt's
president Gamal Abdel Nasser in the 1950s. He was imprisoned

several times and hanged in 1966. His execution made him the
paragon martyr of modern Islamism.

Qutb's Islamist handbook *Milestones* appeared in 1964. In it
he developed the concept of *jahiliyya*, which originally simply
meant the pre-Islamic world of pagan ignorance before the
Qur'anic revelation. Qutb applied it not only to all of Western
civilization but turned it radically against the *umma*, the worldwide community of orthodox Muslims. Muslim societies in the
present stood accused of being not Islamic but *jahili*, 'impious'
or even 'infidel'. This is a grave charge to make against any
born Muslim. It identifies him as an apostate unbeliever liable
to the death penalty.

Qutb's *jahiliyya* theory segregates the Islamists of genuine
faith from the majority of counterfeit Muslims. There is a similarity to Kierkegaard here. Qutb's separation of true faith from
mere outward conformity draws the same line we saw in
Kierkegaard's attack on Christendom. Qutb takes his separatism
to grimmer political extreme.

But who are the genuine Islamists? This is the nub of Qutb's
argument for an existentially valid Islam. Islam lies in ruins
because Muslims have fallen into the snare of *jahiliyya*. Qutb
prescribes a return to the experience of hearing the Qur'an, as it
was originally delivered, as 'war bulletins'. It means choosing
once again to be among the Prophet's first followers. This is not
a going back to the remote past but a claim to witnessing Islam
as it truly is, eternally present in its coming-to-be.

Jahiliyya is a constant threat of lapse into disbelief which can
occur at any time. It is confronted in *jihad*, in sacred war, by
eternal Islam unlimited to time or territory. *Jihad* is the only
instruction needed for Islamists to follow in the footsteps of the
first Muslims, 'who once changed the course of human history
in the direction ordained by God'. Qutb declares: 'I have written

Milestones for this vanguard, which I consider to be a waiting reality about to be materialized.'[20] Those in the vanguard who heed God's call will be led to their predestined end, 'whatever this end may be':

> Then they will not be anxious, while traversing this road forever paved with skulls and limbs and blood and sweat, to find help and victory, or desirous that the decision between the truth and falsehood be made on this earth.[21]

Islamism is often mistaken for a fundamentalist rejection of modernity, but Qutb clearly favours a modern Islamist renaissance. He advises pious Muslims to reclaim technology from the West which has benefited long enough from advances originally due to Islamic science. Technology in his view is a neutral and value-free asset that Muslims should dissociate from Western atheism which has contaminated science. Qutb agitated for a modernizing Islamist vanguard directed as much against archaic Islam as against the West. It is no surprise to find technologically educated militants in Al-Qaeda's first rank.

Sayyid Qutb's tour of America served only to harden his contempt for a shallow 'pagan civilization' of jazz and impious liberalism. The Cairo intellectual, a forty-three-year-old celibate virgin, seemed especially troubled by bold-faced American females with lavish breasts and smooth legs. Qutb's offended modesty has passed down to the Al-Qaeda terrorists.

Fifth thought experiment

Is there an Islamist existentialism?

There is a Christian existentialism. So too there are identifiable forms of Jewish, Hindu, Buddhist or indeed Muslim existentialism. But the question of Islamist existentialism implies a *terrorist* dimension. Is terrorism compatible with existentialist belief?

There is certainly an existential core to Qutb's Islamist belief. One resemblance to Kierkegaard has already been noted. Here is another more profound likeness. Kierkegaard speaks of a 'leap of faith'. We can only come to the unknown of faith by surrender of human reason. We are back with Pascal's fideism. The only proof I can have of faith is its genuineness. Something beyond all comprehension has irrupted into my existence and spoken to me of infinite difference. I am made different by this experience of answering to the *else* of infinite Being. Faith is now the expression of my innermost being. It is indeed *who* I am.

We find Qutb doing much the same. He puts a limit to *ijtihad* – 'interpretative reason' – which had been the cornerstone of Islamic philosophy in its golden age. Qutb sidesteps reason. Reason can mislead the mind into scepticism and paralyse the will to action. It suffices to heed God's call in the Qur'an. That alone is the choice of freedom which can release 'man from servitude to man'. The Qur'an is at once both Divine Reason and the unknown of faith to which human reason must limit itself. Qutb thereby relieves the Islamist of any burden of interpretation by prescribing literal faith.

A Muslim's freedom of action rests solely on *hakimiyya* or the sovereignty of God. It therefore follows that a Muslim in his innermost being exists in defiance of the hostile *jahiliyya* world that surrounds and threatens him. He is inevitably called to *jihad* as a *fard'ain* (an individual obligation) that a true Muslim cannot neglect.

Qutb goes further. He shifts the question of being Muslim to the decisive status of being human. If Islam is the only true faith, then the only proper foundation of humanity is to be genuinely Muslim. The danger is that others who are not purely Islamist may be judged insufficiently human – with consequences by now well-known.

Making a cult of experience

I have described a position of fundamentalist faith which philosophers of ethics call *decisionism*. Decisionism rejects any reasoned 'abstract' morality and stakes its claim to ethical good faith on a direct appeal to the inner truth of one's conscience as the sole arbiter of right action. It is a private creed which need not take religious form – it can even be atheist – but often justifies itself by professing to authentic Islamist or Christian or other forms of purist belief.

Decisionism is at the heart of the Islamist's choice of terrorism as an individual act of worship. It has no concern for the approval of the orthodox majority. The Islamist believes himself called to witness for the faith neglected by mundane Muslims.

Existentialism technically has no remedy against decisionism because existence itself cannot limit choice. Sartre accepts that 'whenever a man chooses his purpose and his commitment in all clearness and in all sincerity, whatever that purpose may be, it is impossible to prefer another for him'.[22]

The problem of decisionism is not exclusive to existentialism but haunts all philosophies of ethics. It can be posed as a question of what decides me on a course of action. What convinces me that my choice of action is morally 'good'? Because it is God's will? Or because it is authorized by tradition or social consensus? Or simply, in the end, because I *think* it is good? How do I know I am acting in 'good faith'? The problem is acute for religious existentialists; but even sceptical or atheist existentialists, unburdened by any transcendental faith, must reply to the question, 'What makes me think I am authentic?'

This quest for authenticity easily falls prey to the *experience mystique*. Believers may be tempted to make a mystique out of the experience of being 'truly in oneself' a Muslim, a Christian, a Jew or whatever else. An aura of cult attaches itself to the experience of authenticity for its own sake.

The experience mystique is a thorn in the flesh of all religious existentialists. I can find it in Sartre's existential Catholic opponent Gabriel Marcel, who speaks of 'witnessing' for the inner experience of faith. It is glaringly and self-destructively evident in the case of the Jewish-Christian Simone Weil (1909–43). It compelled the philosopher Martin Buber (1878–1965) to ask his audience of Zionist students in 1910, 'Jews, why do we call ourselves Jews?' It led the Russian Orthodox existentialist Nikolai Berdyaev (1874–1948) away from revolutionary Marxism to messianic Christianity as the 'maximum experience' of human existence.

Of course, experience is the only answer to the question,

'What is it like (for instance) to *be* a Christian?' But the trouble is that religious experience implies a sustaining *doctrine*. Doctrine at some level requires the assent of reason which is vulnerable to doubt. The experience mystique attempts to silence doubt by desiring to *feel* the exceptional truth that doctrine alone cannot guarantee. An experiencer of faith risks becoming unreasonably dogmatic in the effort to withstand criticisms of doctrine. Experience is not defending doctrine so much as its own existential conviction of being in 'good faith'. This can lead to fundamentalism.

Fundamentalism is not unique to a fanatical minority but essential to any religion which believes itself in sole possession of the truth. A religion cannot afford to jeopardize that belief by diluting its fundamental doctrines. Every religion is in this sense 'fundamentalist'.

Paul Tillich (1886–1965) wrestled all his life with the existential problem of doctrine. Can the modern experience of belief, with all its besetting doubts, find credible answers in Luther's doctrine of 'justification by faith'? Tillich's chief work *Systematic Theology* (1951–63), sets up a dialogue in which the questions asked by free human reason (*autonomy*) are preparations for the answers given in Christian revelation (*theonomy*). Tillich resorts to Kierkegaard's acknowledgement that the absurdity of faith must in the end transcend the limits of reason. It must be said that Tillich doubted the viability of any systematic answer to God's reality – which has led some to claim him wrongly as a theologian of the 'God is dead' school.

Cardinal John Henry Newman (1801–90), a near contemporary of Kierkegaard, proposed his own solution to the question of doctrine. Newman belongs to a native breed of English existentialists. His faith evolved in steps. He abandoned Calvinist fundamentalism after a severe spiritual crisis in his early youth but retained a fearful abhorrence of the Roman Catholic papacy. He turned to Anglicanism, took Holy Orders, and became a famous reform activist of the Tractarian or Oxford Movement. This God-intoxicated dissenter finally converted to Catholicism and was ordained a priest at the age of forty-six.

Newman tackled the perennial existentialist question of 'good faith' in the *Grammar of Assent* (1870). How do Christians give reasonable assent to the doctrines of Scripture? Newman recognized that in practice most Christians do not base their assurance of faith on well-reasoned logical proofs. Their assent results instead from the workings of what Newman calls the *illative sense*. (Illative, a grammatical term, signifies 'motion towards', as in expressions like 'therefore', 'consequently', 'it follows that'.) Newman's illative sense describes a 'mental mosaic' by which innumerable small possibilities accumulate and tend towards certitude. This is the 'grammar' which finds voice in a religious act of unconditional assent.

Newman's own evolution made him keenly sensitive to the development of Christian doctrine. It was crucial to him that current Christian doctrines must be shown identical to those of the original apostolic age, even though they have developed and undergone change. Newman's theory is that any vital idea – be it political, logical, historical, ethical or scientific – must by nature develop in the minds which seek its application in reality. Newman's view of evolutionary doctrine – a *living* Christianity – is of immense importance to modern theology. It allows for the possibility that faith in doctrine does have a basis in reason, because both doctrine and reason are necessarily going to change over time. Scientific findings and those of theology evolve in parallel, each with its own distinct existential reality, and need not enter into conflict.

Newman's humanely reasoned theology offers possible alterations to the Vatican's entrenched dogmas against women's ordination, marriage for the clergy, divorce, contraception and abortion. Islam too, like Roman Catholicism, must urgently decide on what is essential to redemptive faith and what is expendable dogmatic chaff.

But how far down the road of expedience can religion dare to go in shedding doctrine?

Rudolf Bultmann (1884–1976), another German Protestant theologian, has gone furthest to adapt Christianity to a disbelieving secular world. He concedes that the Gospel texts are not reliable history. It does not matter to him whether they are fact or myth. Their message is what essentially counts. Bultmann proposes faith in a 'demythologized' Christianity. Only a purely existential account can make sense of the Gospels' message in our time.

But what is the original Gospel 'message'? It is Christ's resurrection, taken as fact not myth. I do not see much consolation for the believer in Bultmann's dwindled message which declares this fact an expendable myth.

A parable on suicide

I know of no existing world religion that condones suicide. Islam is no exception. Islamists get round this prohibition by playing on the double sense of *shahid*, which can mean both 'martyr' and 'witness'. Suicide bombers are not suicides but performers of *istishhad* or 'self-martyrdom'.

What sense does suicide have for the atheist? There is no divine authority to forbid the atheist's choice of suicide. Is there any earthly reason that could?

Albert Camus (1913–60) took on the challenge of finding an answer to suicide from an atheist perspective: 'There is but one truly serious philosophical problem, and that is suicide. Judging whether life is or is not worth living amounts to answering the fundamental question of philosophy.'[23] These are the opening sentences of Camus' *The Myth of Sisyphus*, published in 1942, when Nazi Germany had occupied France. It seems an odd time to pose such a dark problem. Courageous individuals like Camus himself joined the French Resistance to the Occupation. He edited an underground resistance news-sheet, which later became the Parisian daily *Combat*, at considerable personal risk. One might have expected him to write something more optimistic than thoughts on suicide. But it is typical of existentialists to ask awkward questions at unpropitious moments. Camus sensed that an underlying nihilism had pervaded Europe and resulted in totalitarian ideologies.

Camus was a being of fiercely independent rectitude opposed to all ideological labels. He knew hardship as the son of poor immigrant *pied-noir* colonists in Algeria and always remained sensitive to his homeland's tragic history. Apprenticed in journalism, Camus preferred the essay, novel or play to weighty theoretical tomes. His writings are admirably free of jargon; but one special term, 'the absurd', bears his trademark. The absurd concerns two related but incompatible states of existence. The first refers to the fact that human existence cannot expect to have meaning in a meaningless universe. Existence is absurd. The second and more important point for Camus is that we must choose to live absurdly, fully conscious of being without sense, but never surrender in despair to the senseless. 'The absurd has meaning only in so far as it is not agreed to.'[24] The absurd person is forbidden suicide on pain of surrendering to absurdity.

Camus remarks that 'a reason for living is also an excellent reason for dying'.[25] Loyalty to country, for instance, or struggle for national independence or defence of one's family will each give a good reason for living – and for dying. There was plenty evidence of that in 1942. But suicide asks the untimely question: 'What is the meaning of life? How do I resolve that in order to live?' Camus arrives at an answer consistent with the absurd. Life need not have a meaning to be lived. On the contrary, he says, 'it will be lived all the better if it has no meaning'.[26]

Camus' ethic is a clear and simple one of endurance. One must not yield to despair. He calls this a blessing of 'Mediterranean light', which enlightens us to bear the unbearable with joy rather than gloom. He echoes Nietzsche's exultation of healthy 'noonday light'.

Camus ends his essay on suicide with the ancient Greek myth of Sisyphus. Sisyphus was condemned to eternal punishment for defying the gods. They sentenced him to the ceaseless task of rolling a huge stone to the top of a mountain, whence it would roll back down again of its own weight. Nothing would seem more dreadful to the gods than this futile and hopeless labour.

I take Camus' parable to mean that the real crime of Sisyphus was his denial of the gods. His crime was atheism. The rock which he shoulders uphill each day, only to face it again the next, is nothing else than the weight of absurdity that everyone must bear. But there is also a moment when Sisyphus triumphs over the senseless. As he descends wearily from the summit, in that time of pause, he gains his 'hour of consciousness' and knows himself superior to his fate:

This universe henceforth without a master seems to him neither sterile nor futile. Each atom of that stone, each mineral flake of that night-filled mountain, in itself forms a world. The struggle itself towards the heights is enough to fill a man's heart. One must imagine Sisyphus happy.[27]

I catch allusions to Kierkegaard's 'joyful repetition' and Nietzsche's 'eternal recurrence' in Camus' picture of a happy Sisyphus.

What would Camus make of Islamist *istishhad*? I think it would appear understandable to him but inexcusable as suicide. The martyr agrees to absurdity by surrendering to it.

The existentialist is rescued from suicide by acknowledging that faith in life must grow all the more acute in its vigilant awareness of the absurd. Atheism separates Camus from Kierkegaard; but they are reunited in this paradox of the 'leap of faith' *into* the absurd and also *beyond* it. Kierkegaard adds the further proviso of modesty: no one is ever assured of being in 'good faith'. Kierkegaard does not support the fundamentalist notion of 'justified belief' which is tantamount to knowing God's intention. A sense of the absurdity of faith safeguards the existentialist against self-righteous fanaticism.

Camus and Sartre had become friends during the wartime Resistance. It was always an edgy friendship which came unstuck in 1952 when Camus' book *The Rebel* attacked the totalitarian element in Marxism. Sartre replied with a ferocious editorial in his journal *Les Temps Modernes* which accused Camus of disloyalty to the oppressed. 'What should I do?' Camus said. 'Go smash his face in? The guy's too small.' It would have been an interesting match, since, apparently, Sartre had taken boxing lessons.

Interlude

Husserl: the midnight of modernity

> The question of Husserl . . . is the question of the origin of the
> world. It is, so to speak, the question implied in myths, reli-
> gions, theologies and ontologies.
>
> *Paul Ricouer* [28]
>
> 'What makes the desert beautiful,' said the little prince, 'is that
> somewhere it hides a well . . .'
>
> *Antoine de Saint-Exupéry* [29]

Jean-Paul Sartre said in a 1945 lecture that existentialism is the
'most austere' of all teachings, 'intended strictly for technicians
and philosophers'. Yet he also claimed that existentialism 'can
easily be defined'.[30] Both claims are true. He had in mind
Edmund Husserl's technically demanding philosophy when
speaking of existentialism's austerity. Some acquaintance with
Husserl's 'science of phenomenology' is useful if we are to
understand twentieth-century existentialism.

Edmund Husserl (1859–1938), a Jew born in Austrian
Moravia, converted to Lutheranism at the age of twenty-seven
in 1886, a procedure of assimilation into Austro-German society required at the time for a university career. Husserl came to

philosophy by way of mathematics. His investigations settled on a topical issue hotly contested in the avant-garde circles of mathematicians, logicians and experimental psychologists. Are the foundations of mathematics grounded in the psychological laws that govern the mind or in the pure formal laws of logic whose necessity we can only intuit? This might seem a dry, abstract question of specialist interest. But as the century turned, it became a question of crisis in science as the mathematical laws of Newton's physics appeared overthrown by the discovery of relativity and quantum indeterminacy.

Husserl came to the insight that proper investigation into the groundings of mathematics and logic must start from analysis of the experience which precedes any formal thinking. He was led to a method of quizzing the way we experience things as immediately present to our consciousness. In short, Husserl looks into consciousness itself 'caught in the act' of actually perceiving reality. Can we isolate the act of perception from that which appears to it? This study he called phenomenology, which derives from the Greek, *phainomai*, 'appear' or 'show'.

The shadow of dark times twice fell across Husserl's tranquil academic pursuit. The First World War, in which his son died in action, made it clear to him that the values of European culture had collapsed. Hitler was the second catastrophe. Nazi racial doctrine declared Husserl a Jew outlawed from public life and teaching. Husserl fought back in old age and illness by speaking in defence of scientific enlightenment and the freedom of philosophy. His final address in 1935 is to those who lament that 'science has nothing to tell us in our vital need'. His answer to this 'crisis of science' in dark times is a profoundly existential one.

Sixth thought experiment

A meditation on consciousness

Husserl's phenomenology begins with a simple question. 'What is taken for real?' The answer is equally simple: 'That which is directly given to us.' We cannot do otherwise than perceive things 'as they are' in a world already given to us and taken for granted. We take our awareness of the world as *evidence* of it. This is the unacknowledged presupposition on which our faith in reality is secured. Husserl calls this our 'natural attitude', a basic pre-scientific naivety from which we all start.

We might at this stage already foresee Husserl's next question: 'Is there something mistaken in our natural attitude to perceiving reality?' It is a question answered 'yes' by the opposing traditions of religion and science. Religion says that our grasp on things must surrender to a higher spiritual or transcendental truth. Our senses and emotions are reduced to errors, illusions or in some cases sins. Science puts our commonly held views in doubt. Our senses and emotions which ordinarily mislead us into errors of fact and prejudices must be neutralized by impersonal experiment. Science arrives at the indubitable truth of things by its method of reductionism. This means reducing all phenomena to their bottom-line factual explanation. So that, for example, 'red is nothing but light of a certain wave length'; or 'a smile is nothing but contractions of the circumoral muscles'.

The spiritual exercises of religion and the materialist mechanics of science agree on this one point – reality is different to what we naturally suppose it to be. Both might justifiably be said fundamentalist in their reductions of reality to absolute certainty. But this is not our everyday experience of the world. 'Red' is for us a transient attribute of wine or lips or a sunset; a smile is a possibility of someone's greeting or irony or contempt. We perceive *variations* that have no absolute constancy.

Husserl enters on the side of experience. The natural attitude is not mistaken but incomplete. Husserl offers us another meditation on science in which consciousness must take full account of the 'life-world', as he calls it.

Modern sceptical philosophy, ever since Descartes, had correctly identified the problem of subjectivity. Subjective experience can indeed misinterpret evidence and lead us astray. Subjectivity only appears clear to itself when it pulls away from its roots in a taken-for-granted world. The 'I' is then exposed as that which naturally infers that 'things are as they appear to be'. In other words, the 'I' becomes an object of conscious lesson to itself. It can be studied as an appearance that maintains the appearance of all other things in the world. This is what happens when Descartes says 'I think therefore I am.' *I think* is theoretically divorced from existence so that the process can begin of verifying what is undoubtedly and 'really true'. And this is the high road to reductionism.

Husserl agrees that sceptical reduction is essential. We must recognize the fact that *pre-givenness* is something granted to the world by consciousness and can be questioned. But he does not consent to the current scientific practice of reduction which discards natural experience. Instead, he insists on the original sense of reduction, *reducere* in Latin, which means 'to bring or lead back'. His meditational reduction 'leads back' to the fullness of things experienced in consciousness. How does this work?

I learn to see the world differently by taking note of the act of consciousness as it beams towards an object. This is a change in my way of seeing things which leads me to envisage the object not in itself, as 'given', but in accordance with the act of consciousness which bears it. I do not alter the world in this way. I do not deny its existence. I do not make it an invention of my consciousness. But I enlarge my field of experience by intensifying it, by allowing the world another dimension, free of ordinary pre-givenness. I get back to my experience in another light. It is the same world; but I am the one transformed by regaining it.

There is a problem in attending to the act of consciousness. Anyone who has ever tried to meditate will know that attention wavers. So too, in Husserl's reduction, I 'wobble' in keeping my sights steady on the *perceptual act* itself. I am ensnared by the object I admire, say, a rose, the complexity of its varied petals, its colour darkening as a cloud passes overhead. I must constantly renew my effort to retain the act of consciousness as it actually occurs, and not slip back into my absorption in the object. I will soon realize that there can never be a complete coincidence of the two. A time lag, even if only for a moment, intrudes between the object perceived and the perceptual act of consciousness.

Husserl understood that time constitutes the 'flow' of consciousness. This is why he introduced the device of *epochè* to stabilize the wavering of attention in time. *Epochè* comes from *epekhô*, 'I stop', by which the ancient Greek Sceptics indicated their suspension of all judgement. Husserl employs *epochè* to 'bracket out' any thought arising from the object which distracts me from my observation of the perceptual act alone. In other words, *epochè* suspends the force by which an object reenters its claim to validity in my field of consciousness. It is this claim to validity – and not the existence of the object – which is put temporarily out of action. The object stays where it is, a fact in the world, but left in suspended animation. *Epochè* serves to guide the meditational reduction over the rapids of time. Husserl states: '. . . through the *epochè*, the gaze of the philosopher in truth first becomes fully free . . . Free of the strongest and most universal, and at the same time most hidden, internal bond, namely, of the pre-givenness of the world.'[31]

Epochè is a liberation of consciousness. It allows us rescue from the fearful sense of being 'thrown' into a predetermined world resistant to meaning. But beware! Reduction by *epochè* is undertaken at one's peril. The effort of suspending the normal givenness of reality can plunge one headlong into vertigo. Husserl acknowledges *epochè*'s risk of leading to the ego's 'null point' and thereby committing a sort of philosophical suicide. *Epochè* parallels the chasm which awaits the misstep of the psychotic. To regain the fullness of reality across this tightrope of meditation demands long effort and discipline.

Husserl asks us to persist in the task of meditation. Its reward will come in shattering the chain of our inviolable attachment to simple reductive *fact*. We are used to thinking of fact as concrete and essence as abstract. Husserl reverses these normal connotations. Fact is instead abstract because it actualizes one possibility alone to the exclusions of all others. Essence proceeds to the concrete by drawing on all the indefinite variations that fact ignores as inessential. I give an example. There are infinite variations of shades of red in the world. Where is the invariant essence of redness – in the glow of a fire, an autumn maple leaf, Van Gogh's hair, a bloodstain, or a glass of claret? It is concretely identified in all of them – and in others more than I can number. Where does the variable of redness come from? Where does it stabilize? When does it 'stop' to become the fact of *this* red and not *that* one?

There is an existentialist *physics*, yet to be developed, behind Husserl's method of meditational reduction.

Husserl is more concerned with describing the philosophical consequences of his method than in detailing the practice of *epochè* meditation. It can be extracted by patient devotion to his texts. There is aid in consulting Eastern exercises which provide a variety of 'contemplative technologies'. The Buddhist tradition of *Samatha*, literally meaning *quiescence,* offers attentional training devised to counteract the hindrances of excitation and laxity. The discipline of *Samatha* is not bound to any one religious or philosophical creed. Zen, in its Chinese Ch'an origin, recommends freezing the mind by raising the *hua t'ou* or 'doubt sensation': 'a special type of doubt – a doubt without content – or more succinctly, the pure sensation of "doubt" per se . . . like a great mass or load weighing upon one's mind.'[32] This is a helpful approximation to *epochè* which suspends the validity of the world's pre-givenness. The aim of Eastern contemplative techniques is similarly to bring all thought to a halt in order to display the fundamental workings of consciousness itself.

The life-world of consciousness

Husserl's method of *epochè* reduction demands individual practice. Reduction cannot dispose of its criterion of internal intuitive evidence. This is because we are each of us rooted in our own temporality, literally *temporary*, in our unique rhythms of being concretely here and now. No one can share in that moment in which I am. We know from ordinary experience that the mind inclines to inward isolation. But this is not the whole story.

The mind is unsettled by its physical states. It is embodied. It is always physically in question. My natural tendency to split the mind from body is already evident in saying 'I have a body', and more often than not as an encumbrance whose misbehaviours I must bear. I can be led by extreme to reject this material opacity of the body, and of things in general, to seek a *dis*incarnate higher fact in religion or science. I can become convinced to treat the physical conditions of being as enemies, as deceivers, to be subdued by spiritual or scientific reductions.

Husserl asks: 'Who' is this 'I' that 'has' a body?

The indispensable support in my labour to be human is my body. I do not have a body, I *am* my lived body. What does it signify in practice to be a lived body? It gives us our one assurance that the world really is there in its shared pre-givenness. I can make nothing of myself without others. I realize myself in the plural of human *being*. I can find in my lived body that there is an entire collective body of consciousness, a life-world, composed of manifold surrounding worlds. Husserl, in his crisis years of Hitlerian darkness, began investigating diverse kinds of surrounding human worlds – among them the world of early childhood, the world of the 'mature' person as 'normal', the world of 'primitive' peoples, the world of the abnormal, the world of the sick – over against the surrounding worlds belonging to animals.

Husserl believed that meditation can never be purely solitary. It is, and must be, complemented by an inter-subjective sharing of the life-world:

> . . . let us turn our attention to the fact that in our continuously flowing world-perceiving we are not isolated but rather have, within it, contact with other human beings. Each one has his perceptions, his presentifications, his harmonious experiences, devaluation of his certainties into mere possibilities, doubts, questions, illusions. But in *living with one another* each one can take part in the life of the others. Thus in general the world exists not only for isolated men but for the community of men; and this is due to the fact that even what is straightforwardly perceptual is communalized.[33]

What does Husserl mean by 'communalized'? He is aiming at two desirable but unrealized goals of conscious community. It might be objected that intersubjective communities already plentifully exist. Scientists would say that they form such a working community. So also those practising religion, philosophy, politics, law, and so on, would claim to be similar intersubjective communities. The problem is that they are antagonistic or atomized specialities in our life-world, and so to speak, *un*-communalized.

Husserl's goal of overcoming the barrier of *defective* science is envisaged in his second objective. He aims at the ethical dimension of experiencing others in their singularity. Consciousness enters into an I-to-I relation by way of intersubjective empathy. Husserl is not advocating a vaguely pious 'empathy' but one that keeps strictly to the rigours of *epochè*. It respects the other's irreducible difference, acknowledges the other's difficulties, but also benefits from other's accumulated experience.

Husserl was in fact struggling against Hitler's idea of community which isolates itself in race and thereby falsifies the transmission of history. How do we take proper account of our *place* in history? We find ourselves in history because we meet others there. But the making of history will often seem to elude the individual. The individual's situation in history will be a central existential question addressed by Jean-Paul Sartre:

> But if History escapes me, this is not because I do not make it; it is because the other is making it as well.
>
> . . . it is not true that History appears to us an entirely alien force. Each day with our own hands we make it something other than what we believe we are making it, and History, backfiring, makes us other than we believe ourselves to be or to become.[34]

Interlude

Heidegger: the maverick philosopher

> The future alone will judge which was the true Germany in
> 1933, and who were the true Germans – those who subscribe to
> the more or less materialistic-mythical racial prejudices of the
> day, or those Germans pure in heart and mind, heirs to the
> great Germans of the past whose traditions they revere and per-
> petuate.
>
> *Edmund Husserl* [35]

Martin Heidegger (1889–1976) was born in Swabia, the
Catholic heartland of Germany. He entered a Jesuit seminary
before training in theology at the University of Freiburg in
1909. Heidegger abandoned Catholicism in 1919 but always
remained secretly an 'apostate believer'. He followed the agnostic principle that one's personal faith is irrelevant to the science
of philosophy.

Heidegger benefits more than other twentieth-century
philosophers from an exceptionally rich philosophical culture.
An intense apprenticeship equipped him with a deep grounding
in Western thinking. The ancient Greek pre-Socratics are as
familiar to him as the medieval scholastics, Descartes, Kant,

Hegel and Karl Marx, the modernist logicians and even the Eastern philosophies of Buddhism and Shinto. Kierkegaard and Nietzsche were his existential turning points; but the deepest influence on him was the recondite science of phenomenology pioneered by Edmund Husserl.

Heidegger served as Husserl's right-hand assistant from 1919 to 1923 at Freiburg University. But then the apprentice defected from the ranks of phenomenology to pursue his own maverick route.

Heidegger assumed the rectorship of Freiburg University on 21 April 1933. To accept that post, in the very year that Hitler was elected Chancellor of Germany, made Heidegger a functionary of the incoming Nazi regime. He pledged his admiration for the Führer on a number of public occasions, in official speeches and articles.

So, why did he choose Hitler? This question will forever darken any interest in Heidegger's philosophy. Is it another example of existentialism 'going wrong'?

Heidegger's choice must be understood as unique in the pantheon of twentieth-century existentialists. Yet none of the resolutely anti-Nazi existentialists believe that Heidegger's philosophy should be disqualified from our serious attention. Why is this? It is not a matter of exonerating him but of grasping a process of thought which surpasses its original thinker's error. To be sure, it remains an impermissible error, all the more astounding for what is judged independently right in the philosophy itself.

Heidegger presents a strange case of quarantined thought. What is so admirable about Heidegger's thought that it can withstand, *in spite of,* his choice?

I should emphasize that Heidegger resigned from the rectorship in February 1934, after barely nine months in office, and before Hitler claimed absolute dictatorship in August 1934. Had the philosopher come to recognize his grave error? No word of apology or remorse or explanation was ever heard from him. The episode remains shrouded in enigma.

I think a clue may be found in Heidegger's rectorship inauguration speech. He ended not with the formulaic 'Heil Hitler!' but with a quotation from Plato's *Republic*: 'All great things stand in peril.' What 'peril' is it that speaks ancient Greek in the midst of declared allegiance to Hitler? We must try to discover what peril Heidegger bears in mind, not just for the 1930s but beyond, for the post-War nuclear age of advanced technology.

Heidegger conducted a passionate love affair with a beautiful and 'frighteningly intelligent' Jewish student, Hannah Arendt, at Marburg University in 1924. She was eighteen and he, many years her senior, was married and had two sons. He kept their liaison secret by contriving arcane tram-routes and rendezvous schemes. Arendt asks in a poem she wrote at the time:

> Why do you give me your hand
> Shyly, as if it were a secret?
> Are you from such a distant land
> That you do not know our wine?

She had reason later to entitle Heidegger 'the secret king of philosophy'.

Seventh thought experiment

The question of Being

> Yet being – what is being? It 'is' It itself. The thinking that is to
> come must learn to experience that and to say it. 'Being' – that
> is not God and not a cosmic ground. Being is essentially farther
> than all beings and is yet nearer to the human being than every
> being, be it a rock, a beast, a work of art, a machine, be it an
> angel or God. Being is the nearest. Yet the near remains farthest
> from the human being.
>
> *Martin Heidegger*[36]

Being and Time, Heidegger's enigmatic masterwork of 1927,
defies categorization. It was the beginning of Heidegger's solitary path to his lifetime's question of Being: *What is 'is'?*

To ask what is 'is' risks falling into nonsense. What is the
point of vexing us with a mere usage of grammar? 'Is' is a verb –
and that's all there is to it.

But not for Heidegger. Our situation in history today is one
of grave peril which has resulted from what Heidegger calls our
'forgetting of Being'. What does he mean? Why does the question of Being imperil us?

Heidegger is fully aware of the absurdity that strikes us in his question. Being is that which we commonly ascribe to things. We say 'they are' and set to work practically on them. But something was forgotten in the long history of taking 'is' for granted. We have by now forgotten that *being* itself remains indefinable as a thing. Being is not *a* being. Being is instead that which allows the sum total of beings to be *present* but does not identify itself with any of them. It cannot have the identity which occurs when I assert an existence, 'this is a tree', but is never that one or any other thing I can name.

In fact, we might rightly conclude that Being is *not*.

What is this *not* by which everything else is made to appear? Heidegger puts it another way. 'Why are there things rather than nothing?' He is provoking us to see the 'isness' that appears from *no*-thing. He does not expect the technically ready-made answers – that the 'world is' by God's creation from nothing or by cosmic evolution. These and other likely answers are forgetfulness that Being is no thing. Religion, philosophy and science have long prepared our amnesia of Being and must be rolled back to the unanswered question of what is is. If we can begin to grasp that question, Heidegger says, we are on the right track to overcoming our amnesia. We must go back counter-clockwise and undo the two-and-a-half-thousand-year habits of mind which have totally concealed Being from us.

A brief lesson on metaphysics

The question of Being was first voiced by the Greek pre-Socratic thinkers of the fifth century BC. It was an expression of authentic wonder at that moment, Heidegger says, but already threatened by the ambiguity of the Greek word *on* which could mean either 'to be' in the infinitive sense or signify just 'a being' or also a higher 'supreme' being.

Thinking at once went off in two complementary directions. Plato first distinguished between sense-perceived beings and the higher supra-sensible Ideas which are the eternally true forms of being. Aristotle next devised the 'great chain of being' which ascends from the lowest inanimate matter to higher forms of being until reaching the uncaused First Cause, the supreme Being, or the unseen God. Both these views conspire to reduce Being to an accurate perception of beings, in short, to a knowledge primarily true to the human mind. Medieval theology followed on the path of Plato, and especially Aristotle, under the guidance of early Islamic scholarship.

We are proceeding in the first steps of *metaphysics* as it turns away from Being. Metaphysics seeks to gain mastery of the 'real reality' which is believed to stand behind our ordinary and often misleading confrontations with sensory experience.

Heidegger wishes us to see that Being is not God or existent beings, and least of all what we can master by our dominance over things. But this is the fork in the path that metaphysics next took.

Descartes is the signpost to modern scientific verification. Truth is no longer referred to any being higher than the rational human subject in face of verifiable objects. We can only speak of what is true to fact. Hume, Kant and other sceptics after Descartes repudiated the metaphysical notion that anything can be known outside the given natural world. Not only does the Supreme Being retreat from this landscape of scepticism but so too does the question of Being vanish altogether. But scepticism cannot give an account of what exactly secures the human subject to a knowledge of reality. Science alone promises a domain of certitude that metaphysics pursued in vain.

Metaphysics is not eliminated in this process of scientific ascendancy but signs over its legacy of 'real reality' to science. This is Heidegger's point. Metaphysics is not the pre-history of science but its present currency.

Metaphysics seemed finally done to death by Nietzsche's death of God. 'God' is just a convenient term for the supremacy of ideas on which the values of Western civilization had hitherto been founded. That foundation has collapsed. The twentieth century ran ahead inexorably to our dominant Will to Power over all beings classified as things for technological appliance.

Heidegger gives the name 'nihilism' to this dehumanization of human *being* in its own descent to technological object. But there is more to this peril of nihilism. The displacement of Being from our awareness is the end from which all of Western metaphysics starts off. I repeat: nihilism is not the end *to which* Western thinking has led but an end *from which* it begins. It is an end, so to speak, always now beginning.

We normally think of metaphysics as a mode of airy speculation discarded in the advance of science. Heidegger thinks counter-clockwise to progress. Metaphysics does not 'pass away' from history but is itself the history of science which conceals Being from us.

Technology beyond good and evil

Let us consider again Sayyid Qutb's Islamist theory in this Heideggerian light. Qutb supposed that technology is a neutral and value-free scientific gain. Technology is admittedly a Western possession, but Qutb claims it can be recuperated by Islamists independently of its Western *jahiliyya* metaphysics. Heidegger's reply would be that Western metaphysics is not a 'speculation' additional to or separable from science. The two are one and the same amnesia. Being is neither God nor its human likeness in mastering things. Qutb falls into the same error that has misled Western thinking into the blind alley of technological extremism. Qutb wants technology handed to the Islamists as a value-free weapon of power. What else has technology ever been in Western hands?

Heidegger is not an ecologist intending to 'save' us from technology. It is too late for that. Our technicity, to use his term, has become second nature to us. His irony is patent. By the time Heidegger came to write on *The Question Concerning Technology* in 1953, the atom bomb had already befallen us. Our annihilation was not an impending fate but had 'already taken place', understood in the sense of the 'end' which Heidegger places at the start of Western metaphysics, an ignition of the Will to Power that cannot be switched off.

Heidegger does not advocate Nietzsche's Will to Power ethic which delivers us to a nihilist technology 'beyond good and evil'. But neither is it possible at this stage to redeem ethics from the ruins of Western values in which metaphysics has been complicit from the start. There is nothing left to redeem from a situation which has come to an end in planetary technology.

Our age troubles us with a great many ethical 'for instances' posed by technology. Here are two easily recognized 'for instances'. For instance, what do we do about euthanasia? Medically or otherwise 'assisted death' on humane grounds is nevertheless suicide. Euthanasia is understandable, defensible and indeed practical. Why should it cause any problem to common sense? Technology has intervened successfully to extend life. It has infiltrated our way of thinking of life to such a degree that *termination* of life now presents itself to us primarily as a technical question. Not so much as a question of 'should it be done?' but 'when should it be done?'

Existentialists agree in rejecting any technical camouflage of suicide – be it euthanasia, Islamist martyrdom or other kind. We have seen Camus' stricture on suicide; but there is something more to consider. The 'end of life' – in which end has the additional sense of final goal – is not a choice in existentialist thinking. A technical end to life in fact deprives us of the sense of choice. We will understand better the existentialist meaning of choice if we turn to the second 'for instance'.

For instance, what do we do about genetics? Nazism had experimented crudely with eugenics. We now have the astonishing technical power to advance the well-being of humanity through embryo research, cloning and genetic engineering. Why should we hesitate to use what is clearly of benefit to millions?

Genetic manipulation is surely the most decisive re-routing of human history. Its momentous significance for us is that *cultural* selection can now replace natural selection. Culture has become a technological feed-back loop permitting us to control our future evolution. Technicians are poised to eradicate illness, alter biological destiny and perhaps even eliminate death – or at least suspend it indefinitely. Science fiction has become fact in everyday life. Technicity is indeed our 'second nature'.

These 'for instances' are the abbreviations of foregone conclusions. The wonder is that so much ethical quandary can be packed into such brevity.

There will no doubt be international debate on these issues, governments will propose legislation to curb 'excesses', protests will be heard from ecologists and other 'sanctity of life' campaigners. But the controversy is already over. It has passed away under media news coverage to yesterday's headlines. Media news-worthiness is by definition almost instantly obsolete, and thereby provides for technology's short-term memory. Technology brings the future into immediate sell-by-date shelf life. We will not be spared what is technically – or as Heidegger says, 'presently' – at hand.

Heidegger is not an anti-science pessimist. He is perfectly clear that 'we can neither repudiate the present-day world of technology as the work of the devil, nor may we nullify it'. Nor does he accept the opinion that 'the world of technology is such that it will simply prevent a liberating leap'. Heidegger invites us to a different meditation on 'the identical essence of Man and Being':

> Not until we turn our thought towards what has already been thought, shall we be employed for what has yet to be thought.[37]

Heidegger's entire life's work on reclaiming Being from oblivion is a summons at the extreme limit of no going back. He does not intend a retreat to the past but a present-day retrieval of our origin in Being. How is that possible?

A therapy of being

Heidegger is struck by the common German word *Dasein*, meaning life, presence or existence. It is composed of two parts, *da*, 'there', and *sein*, 'to be', which gives the sense of 'being-there'. Being-there originally proclaimed the bewildering human encounter of existence with its own fact. We 'stand forth' in awed wonderment, as if heeding some call. But from what? It can only come from Being – from the *thereness* that we are in the first place. Language bears witness to our primordial remembrance of Being.

Heidegger turns our focus away from the philosophers' fixation on the thinking ego, or self-consciousness, towards the *uncon-sciousness* of Being. His attention is on what is *not* thought, on what is forgotten by *Dasein* in its thereness as a human entity. He wishes us to re-sight ourselves on the situation itself of being-there, 'as we are', at a loss in the obviousness of everyday life. Only then perhaps can we recognize our 'deep fall into the inauthenticity' of one-sided technological development. The risk of falling into inauthenticity occurs when the particular *Dasein* surrenders its answerability to the 'they', or as Heidegger puts it, to the everyday self of *Dasein*, which is the public 'they-self'. Idle talk, curiosity, greediness for novelty are characteristics of the public 'they'. There can be no exit from crisis in a situa-tion of literally *distracted being*.

Heidegger is not appraising the human condition from the viewpoint of a moralist or psychologist or sociologist. He is describing a shift to the unconscious obscuring of Being by the very consciousness which takes it for granted. Consciousness cannot be a starting point, because we are *already in it* as a fact of our being-there. We exist normally unmindful of being con-scious. Anxiety, a sudden panicked dread of nothingness that sometimes overcomes us, strips bare our precarious hold on being-there. The world seems to shrink away from us. We are faced at that moment with being nowhere at home in exis-tence. It is a sobering encounter with the disclosure of one's own freedom. I am confronted with the fact of being thrown into an existence which cannot guarantee meaning. What does it mean at that moment to be 'authentically myself'? Authenticity is not an essence I can claim as permanently mine. It must be renewed in preparing me to meet my own death. I experience my freedom by recognizing its finite limit. I exist only 'for the time being'. I am the entity fully aware of passing on to nothingness.

Anxiety, dread, absurdity are only some of the existential fundamentals that open us to Being. There are also plentiful structures of joyful activity. Being is not a matter of dread but a 'call' to our true home in the light of joy.

Human existence has untold scope of possibility in the world. But this vastitude must be narrowed down if there is to be an actualization of possibility. Kierkegaard first introduced the existentialist theme that human existence proceeds in its decisions by *cutting off* possibilities. Heidegger went further to speak of the 'powerlessness of *Dasein*' which shows itself in the withdrawal of certain of its possibilities from being-in-the-world. But it is precisely by withdrawals from its finite bank of possibilities that *Dasein* accedes to power. Our commitment to *limitation* places before us the 'real' graspable potential of a world-design which surpasses the pre-given world 'as it is'.

Our present world-design owes its power uniquely to the withdrawal of other possible worlds. *Dasein*'s choice of self-reduction can no longer allow the world to be but is rather 'surrendered over to one particular world-design, possessed by it, overpowered by it'. I quote here from the existential psychiatrist Ludwig Binswanger who is describing the world view of the schizophrenic. What describes an individual psychotic might also apply to a global loss of mind. Are we risking psychotic closure in a technically designed world – the very one today which seems to promise us limitless possibilities?

Human existence is the product of an oceanic gene pool, evolved by natural selection over millions of years. Beings of genius or with Down's syndrome come up unpredictably in the gene lottery. We are gaining the power to limit, or even eliminate, unpredictable genetic defects and concentrate on perfecting the human fabric. Our choices of human design will inevitably be culturally selective. The gene-pool variables would then become, so to speak, ecologically endangered possibilities. There is no way of foretelling the consequences of proceeding by restrictive decisions towards a vanishing point of no return.

Heidegger gave warning of the intent behind Western metaphysics. Western religion, philosophy and finally science have agreed in *immortalizing our decision to be.* Note well what this says. Decision is itself immortalized, not the 'being' which is thereby reduced to design. The aim of 'not dying' has been our decisive goal from the start. Is it not clear by now what seed of virtual immortality has always been present in human being?

Interlude

Sartre: impresario of existentialism

Pope Pius XII, in his 1950 encyclical *Humani generis*, condemned Sartre for 'terrifying nihilism'. The French Communist Party had similarly pronounced on him. To call down the censure of two such opposed arch-reactionaries must surely count as an enviable triumph for Sartre.

Jean-Paul Sartre is the best-known existentialist. He was one of the very few to accept the existentialist label and advertise himself as such. His technically complex works of philosophy were offset by novels, plays and essays of wider popular appeal. Sartre communicated the image of a thinker at once seriously 'difficult' and yet accessible. He gained celebrity status by being a public intellectual, an implacable critic of French society, a clarion voice for international justice. Sartre added glamour to existentialism by thrusting it into the arena of political engagement and giving it extrovert, combative shape.

Sartre was perhaps too successful in popularizing existentialism. It became a Parisian fashion of the early 1950s, adopted by a disaffected post-war generation who dressed in black, had black thoughts and loitered in dark smoke-filled jazz cellars of the Left Bank. He cannot be blamed for this caricature which still clings to existentialism.

Sartre's existentialism emerges from the dark age of the Nazi Occupation of France. He joined the 'Socialism and Liberty' group in solidarity with the French Resistance. In the Cold War era, as the nuclear superpowers contended for supremacy, Sartre took the position of independent Marxist in tireless support of Third World colonized peoples struggling for liberation.

Sartre went to Germany in 1933 to immerse himself in studies of Husserl and Heidegger. That was in the year when Hitler became Chancellor. Sartre attended some of Heidegger's lecture at Freiburg during the contentious Nazi rectorship period. Sartre later maintained that Heidegger's philosophy stood acquitted of weak-kneed and naïve involvement in Nazism. It was not a defence likely to please Heidegger. He retaliated by writing his formidable 'Letter on Humanism' in 1945–6 which accused Sartre of totally misapprehending the question of Being.

Eighth thought experiment

Freedom and the nothing of consciousness

Sartre's earliest philosophical exercises in the late 1930s focused
on the imagination and the emotions. His grasp of these psychological states reveals a skilful deployment of Husserl's
method. *Nausea*, a novel from that period, illustrates Sartre's
tactical extension of scope. (It should be noted that almost
every existentialist mentioned in this book has produced novels,
plays or poetry.) The novel's anti-hero Roquentin suffers from a
pathological revulsion, a 'nausea', inflicted by the glutinous
'density of things' which oppresses him in the everyday world.
He feels crowded out by the proximity of others and burdened
by the inescapable awareness of his own body. How does one
escape the sheer volume of being that weighs down on one's
consciousness?

This existentialist theme is elaborated in Sartre's monumen-
tal opus, *Being and Nothingness*, of 1943. Husserl appears
enlisted in its subtitle: 'Outline of a Phenomenological
Ontology'. Husserl's description of consciousness impressed
Sartre as giving a profound insight into human freedom.
Consciousness for Husserl is composed purely of *intention*
which is always directed at some object. There can be no

'objectless' consciousness, even if that 'object' is consciousness itself. This gave Sartre the insight that consciousness has no existence apart from things present to it. We are dealing with a phenomenon that only 'is' if something other than itself is. Sartre's abiding principle of human freedom stems from this curious but decisive *inexistence* of consciousness. How does he arrive at that?

Consciousness is the *no-thingness* that occurs in a world compacted of thingness or being. Sartre distinguishes between two opposed states of being. There is *being-in-itself* which characterizes the dense, unconscious state of things that confronts our awareness of them. We might call being-in-itself the existing facts that circumscribe our situation in the world. There is also *being-for-itself* which results from our state of consciousness. Sartre is describing what it is like to 'be' in consciousness. It is not like any materially tangible thing we can grasp but is nevertheless real 'for itself'. Being-for-itself is like seeing oneself in a mirror. One is not in there, and yet not an illusion either – a situation which is only ever encountered in consciousness.

What has this to do with freedom?

Consciousness secures our margin of freedom by virtue of negation. We are free to imagine what is not. It is possible for us to differ from the materially given world on condition that consciousness is no-thing. Consciousness acknowledges what is real by experiencing its own negative state. To give a simple example:

I know that cup is there in front of me because it is *not me*.

I assert the cup's existence. It has undeniable being in itself. But at the same time it is the *not* of consciousness that permits me to comprehend a *difference* of being.

Another example:

My friend Simone is *not* in the café . . .

I had expected her to be there. I had something to tell her. But now the café becomes the place where she is *not*. Everything normally there, the waiters in service, the mirror I glance at, people at other tables, now speaks of her absence like a hole reshaping the café's reality for me. *Not there* can have a very present weight of *thereness*.

Bob Dylan has expressed it well in his song, 'Visions of Johanna':

Louise, she's all right, she's just near,
She's delicate and seems like the mirror
But she makes it all too concise and too clear
That Johanna's not here.

Consciousness brings meaning to the world by interposing this 'shell of nothingness' between itself and the objects of which it is conscious. Without this 'hole', there would only be a non-conscious, undifferentiated plenitude of being-in-itself.

Sartre's point is that consciousness *externalizes* reality. This is the opposite of our commonly held assumption that consciousness 'takes in' reality. We should think of it instead as a projective capacity, like a beam of light, similar to Heidegger's 'clearing of Being' which is not itself a thing *in* being.

But if consciousness is nothingness, where then do we find the self? Where is its place?

Descartes enshrined the commonplace principle that the

self is in essence self-consciousness: 'I think therefore I am.' Sartre denies this. There can be no object 'in' consciousness, and hence no self identical to it. Our view of the self must undergo entire displacement. It too is 'out there', externalized, akin to other objects on which consciousness is projected. The self has no material being-in-itself but only being-for-itself. It is an objective that we realize by our project of being in the world.

We have no fixed place in consciousness. There is consequently no human essence, no so-called 'human nature'. Sartre jealously guards freedom from the trap of essentialism which believes there is a fundamentally unalterable human nature apart from the unstable conditions of history. All talk of nature is an excuse of bad faith to avoid bearing the responsibility for one's choice. I can never be free of the circumstances that are not of my own making; but I can choose to negate that situation, to change it and free myself whenever possible.

Sartre insists that our freedom depends absolutely on this one human peculiarity. Consciousness is not a materially determined thing and is not part of the causal order. Modern science takes for granted that our brains are organically 'wired' for consciousness. It is simply a by-product of our neuro-physiological functions. Proof of this is given by the fact that damage to the nervous system can severely handicap consciousness. Sartre's reply is that the nervous system can be described fully *in itself* but has no being *for itself.* No aspect of matter can ever transcend itself to make known to itself what it is. To put this simply: *How can matter have ideas?* Science leaves this crucial question unanswered. Advances in science must themselves depend on an unexplained free margin of consciousness. A mouse may have a DNA structure very like our own; but it does not have – and cannot have – an idea of DNA.

Sartre vowed a lifelong 'essential love' for Simone de Beauvoir. But they rarely lived together. Sartre had always been close to his mother Anne-Marie – they enjoyed playing piano duets – and he resided with her in an apartment near Saint-Germain-des-Prés from 1946 to 1962. The apartment was twice bombed during the crisis years of the Algerian war (1954–62) in reprisal for Sartre's anti-colonial alignment.

Freedom, the atheist's God

Sartre's position is doggedly atheist. It accords with his uncompromising belief in human freedom. We are responsible 'in the end' – and with this circumstantial proviso – for what we make of ourselves.

Sartre's existentialism appeared in tune with a secular world fashioned after the 'death of God'. It shifted the limelight from an equally modern current of Christian existentialism represented by Karl Jaspers (1883–1969), Jacques Maritain (1882–1973), Gabriel Marcel and others. Maritain argued that atheism is a commitment to a certain viewpoint. It is a choice like any other that one is free to make in this world. I can decide to be an atheist; but my decision does not bestow the status of fact on atheism. Sartre instead passes off atheism as the only natural fact from which to start. This is a betrayal of existentialism's deepest principle of freedom. Marcel also accused

Sartre of betraying existentialism by reducing freedom to an essentialist dogma of human nature.

Sartre's atheism is more complex than his Christian opponents allow.

Pascal and Kierkegaard are the first existentialists to acknowledge the 'God-shaped hole' in the universe. Consciousness seeks constantly for its fulfilment in an essence which transcends it. It wishes to be something more than for-itself. It wishes, in Sartre's words, 'to have the impermeability and infinite density of the in-itself'.[38] The fundamental human project is, in short, 'to be God'. Sartre echoes Pascal in declaring that a comprehension of God comes not from religion or society but 'from the heart'.

The problem is not belief in God but the frustration of human being to arrive at more than itself. The condition of freedom is precisely this recognition of human limit. Freedom determines the extent of my possibility and thereby *limits its value*. My possibility appears to me as the being which at present I lack. I choose because I lack 'something' of value; but this value I seek will always be the incompleteness of my own being. Sartre arrives at the paradoxical definition: *freedom is really synonymous with lack*.

Sartre's idea of freedom seems puzzling. We are apt to think of freedom as unrestricted liberty of action. But he is consistent in identifying the nothingness of one's consciousness with freedom. It is indeed by *lack*, upsurging from freedom, that we can experience the perforation of reality by the *not* of consciousness.

Sartre works from these negatives of consciousness and freedom, as a photographer does, to bring their positives into sight. Do we recognize ourselves in the picture he gives of our desire for a *totality* of being?

I am this specific person. I cannot grasp the total picture of my being in the world because time will change it. I exist in the present, as it seems to slip irretrievably away from me, and as the future draws me into its uncertain terrain of possibilities.

Ninth thought experiment

What is time?

Time is the crucial existential element. Our existence is temporal. Time is the matrix in which 'things happen' for us. But what is time? It is said to fly like an arrow. But where does its flight lead? It is said to flow. But from what source to what end? Time eludes us because we cannot grasp it all at once but only in its tripartite successions of past, present and future.

It seems to us normal that clocks can measure this impermanence of time as if it were something divisible into stable units. We are necessarily misled to conceive of time as really existing. But it is nothing other than our awareness of *being-there*.

We might go further and say that consciousness is 'made' of time. This means we can only attend to what time discloses. Our attention is directed to the presence of being. But there is no such presence except in time-structured consciousness.

The very word itself *presence* indicates our encounter with a state of time. It speaks directly of the here and now. But what is presently in view also implies alterations undergone in the past and possible in the future. Change is fated. Our bigger picture of time assumes this shape of fate in the unrelenting course of history. I am history's actor to the extent of being known to others. But I am only ever found in the *already* present of my story, even as I wonder 'what has become of me?' or 'what will become of me?' I cannot easily catch myself in this process of becoming. It escapes me because my awareness itself consists of time. And time is non-identical presence. *It never coincides with itself.*

Consciousness, in Sartre's view, is 'existentially contaminated' by our emotions. We can see what he means by considering our experience of time. Time lags in boredom. It expands in moods of joy or loss. It shrinks suffocatingly in bouts of anxiety. Emotion takes hold of consciousness and qualifies the duration of time. 'I felt depressed for several days.' But I can always count on time to recover its fixed succession of past, present and future. Perhaps it isn't that I am experiencing time, but the reverse. I could say instead that consciousness is itself being experienced by different states of time.

Sartre and Heidegger, in their different ways, are applying phenomenology to describe the crystallizations of emotion in time. Heidegger calls them the 'existential fundamentals'. Here are some examples:

Anguish is a prime existential fundamental. To ask 'What does it arise from?' is the same as asking when it arises. Anguish typically occurs at a moment of decision. Or, to time it more accurately, when I hesitate to complete my next step into the future. 'I am quitting my job.' I've entered the manager's office to tell him that. I am about to say it – but I don't have to. I can change direction and speak of something else. I am then suspended over a time gulf, clinging to the ledge of a present which is already claimed by an unknown future. It is a moment of indecision which I can only prolong by enduring more suspenseful anguish.

Anguish is this untimely 'in-between' state of anticipated consequence. I feel my weight on time's cross. I am painfully conscious of being the non-being of my own future.

Choice is another well-known existential fundamental. Anguish is often brought on by choice – or by the postponement of choice. Denial of choice can appear to be the means of evading the anxieties of responsibility. 'I didn't choose to be like this. It just happened.' But, as Sartre warns, not choosing is also a choice. I have no option but to choose. Sartre puts it bluntly: 'Choice is nothing other than the being of each human reality.'[39]

Only that which is unconscious of lack can exist in itself as a *thing* without choice. Sartre is perfectly aware of extreme conditions of deprivation which permit little or no choice. But no person even in the most hopeless situation is ever reduced to a thing unconscious of lack, and hence will suffer the consciousness of freedom all the more acutely in the absence of choice.

Decision gives me proof that I have freedom only by surrendering it to time. Consider what is effected time-wise by decision. It allows me freely to change what cannot thereafter be changed. I cannot go back on my decision. My decision takes away the choice I first had. This is the paradox of a real or, so to speak, decisive decision. I exert my resolve on a choice in the present that will disallow it in the future. Decision narrows the scope of the possibility I began with. Real decision is irrevocable because it is time-forwarded. I cannot revisit, recall or reverse it. A decision which can be undecided was never a real decision in the first place.

But I am never done. Another decision will at once come

along. There is no decision to end all decisions – except suicide. But suicide is the possibility that denies itself existence.

A **promise** is a decision which travels ahead to its fulfilment in time. It faces me with the problem of reliability. I commit myself to a certain space of time in which both it and I must prove reliable. I have made time into a story which risks anticipating a positively foretold ending.

What similarities and differences does a promise have to a **vow**? What negative aspects does a promise assume in **vengeance** or a **feud**? Is the humanity of a promise lost in the abstract formality of a **contract**? Or is a contract the dispassionate essence of a promise?

I would ask the reader to perform similar thought experiments on other existential fundamentals. Betrayal, love, sincerity, purpose, mourning, conviction . . . Many more will occur to reward the reader's interest. We are looking to appraise the attitudes, emotions and behaviours which constitute the existential stuff of everyday life.

Tenth thought experiment

Is insanity a loss of consciousness?

Consciousness is existentialism's jewel in the crown. The lucidity of consciousness is always there, always in light, even in the murkiest states of existential perturbation.

But what of insanity?

Abnormally flawed consciousness must surely prove impossibly opaque to existentialism. Insanity is existentially treatable if we keep to the light of existentialism's first principle of consciousness.

Existentialism externalizes consciousness. It is therefore strange but correct to say that 'being out of one's mind' places us rightfully in normality. Insanity is being too much in one's mind, imprisoned therein, without imaginable exit. A disordered mind cannot 'get out' to the reality which normally instructs it. What I lose is not my mind but my possibility of stepping free of it to be other than I am. So it is not my identity which is lost to insanity. On the contrary, identity has never been so empirically resistant to change as it is in estrangement. This is why the insane are said incorrigible. They cannot be made to see that their proofs of reality are 'all in the mind'.

It remains normal to have eccentric or bizarre slants on reality. Most of us are crackpot in some way; and all philosophers certainly are. It is also normal to experience anguish which directs us compellingly towards reality in a normal everyday sense. But the anguish of insanity is not like that. It does not come to one from 'out there' in reality but is a closure from within that has no outcome in time and allows no glimpse of freedom in its walled-up being. What becomes of choice, decision or all other existential fundamentals? Insanity submits them all to the same fate. They no longer point outwards to reality but have collapsed hopelessly inwards as if into some catastrophic black hole which permits no light to escape.

Existentialism seems equipped to describe the terrifying features of insanity. But what can it do to penetrate the Medusa's gaze of madness which apparently turns all existential possibilities to stone?

Existentialism's refusal of the Freudian unconscious

Sartre devotes a chapter to 'Existential Psychoanalysis' in his *Being and Nothingness*. He acknowledges his debt to Freud's pioneering method of analysis. But his own existential psychoanalysis breaks radically with Freud's central theory of the unconscious.

How do we understand the unconscious? Freud's idea is that the unconscious operates in unfathomable secrecy below the level of consciousness. It manifests itself pathologically in symptoms which consciousness denies – and it must deny them, otherwise there would be no symptoms for the analyst to bring to the patient's consciousness.

Freud supposes that patients cannot account for their

symptoms because knowledge of them is repressed by the unconscious. Sartre asks, how can anything be effectively repressed without knowing what needs to be repressed? Is there a knowledge which can exist in ignorance of itself? Surely not. The unconscious must be conscious of that which it represses in order precisely not to be conscious of it. We are left with the puzzle of an unconscious which is unintelligible to itself.

The unconscious is redundant in Sartre's view. Would it not be simpler and truer to say that consciousness has acted all along in *bad faith*? Sartre defines bad faith as our normal capacity for self-deception. I can pretend not to be the one who is telling me a lie. And since I do not recognize the liar's existence as my own, I am therefore unaware of the lie and not responsible for it.

Bad faith is the need we feel to evade the burden of freedom. I would rather be determined by a lie than face the truth. But self-deceit does not get me off the hook of choice. I may choose to believe a self-told lie, or more accurately, choose to *disguise* it from myself to become unconscious of it. But disguise is an option which cannot escape from the orbit of consciousness.

Binswanger, the existentialist Freud

What we perceive are 'first and foremost' not impressions of taste, tone, smell or touch, not even things or objects, but rather, meanings.

Ludwig Binswanger [40]

Sartre ends his outline of existential psychoanalysis in 1943 with an expectation. 'This psychoanalysis has not yet found its Freud.' In fact, a 'Freud' had already come along, unknown to

Sartre. This was the Swiss psychiatrist Ludwig Binswanger (1881–1966) who formulated a new existential analysis.

Binswanger's observations of schizophrenia in the 1920s had convinced him that clinical procedures did not satisfactorily provide a real understanding of the states of consciousness actually experienced by patients. He adopted the methods of phenomenology practised by Husserl and Heidegger to gain a subtler grasp of the patient's inner universe. He paid scrupulous attention to the actual being-in-the-world of mental alienation. What is it really 'like' to undergo the feelings of depersonalization which precede the onset of schizophrenia? What 'sense' is experienced by psychotics in states of delusion and hallucination?

Binswanger proposed that states of mental disorder do have *meaning*. This was heresy to orthodox psychiatry. Is it not precisely the aim of clinical treatment to rid the psychotic of those abnormal 'meanings' which have no basis in reality? To say that one hears 'voices' or is 'made of glass' has no other meaning than a pathological one which requires cure.

Binswanger put in a counter-claim which extended psychiatry's therapeutic frontiers. Even the most senseless, deluded belief still has an *existential* meaning in that person's world. This is based on Husserl's claim for the varied life-worlds of consciousness inclusive of all experiences, unrestricted by any single viewpoint on normality. The existential key must be found to the question, 'What does "the voice of God" mean for this particular psychotic?' The voice is not an object explicable from the world outlook of science or of sane persons. To understand a psychotic's world asks that we uncover the existential reality which makes the phenomenon of God's voice possible.

What estranges us from the 'mentally ill', what makes them appear alien to us, are not single perceptions or ideas, but rather the fact of their imprisonment in a world-design which is enormously restricted because it is ruled by one or a very few themes.[41]

The psychotic's world-design has been reduced to an *invariable* condition. 'The emptier, more simplified, and more constricted the world-design to which an existence has committed itself, the sooner will anxiety appear and the more severe it will be.'[42] Binswanger speaks here of 'commitment' as if mental derangement were somehow a choice. That is precisely, and with apparent lack of sympathy, what he is saying. A modification to one's existential comportment occurs in mental illness, such that being-in-the-world no longer freely relates to its own fact. It is, in Binswanger's own words, a 'self-chosen unfreedom'. A disordered mind surrenders itself to a world of its own structuring – but such a world can only come into being inauthentically by sacrificing one's freedom of understanding to it.

Binswanger's idea of 'self-chosen unfreedom' verges on scandal. It flies in the face of the commonly held scientific view which considers the psychotic mind organically disabled to sustain its own recovery. This is not Binswanger's conclusion. Existential analysis differs from clinical psychopathology 'in that it assiduously ignores the biologically orientated distinction between sick and healthy'. It does not annul that distinction but submits it to Husserl's *epochè*, in other words, suspends it. Existential analysis seeks to grasp the disturbance itself not as a deviation from the norm but rather as the autonomous development of a possibility already potentially present in normal experience.

Binswanger's existential analysis must not be confounded with once-fashionable 'anti-psychiatry'. He does not romanticize the pain of mental disorder but aims to restore the sufferer to freedom from the confines of a disordered world-design. The individual can never be treated as a specimen apart from the being-in-the-world which is fundamental to us all. Existentialists begin from the principle that a disturbed world-design is always a possibility already present in normal experience. Such a commitment to the priority of the world over the individual who is situated in it will have certain consequences. Culture and history must feature as crucial to the wholeness of our life-world in which ill- or well-being finds itself existentially at stake.

Interlude

Fanon: on race and existential deviation

Jews, blacks and other racially characterized persons have been subjected for centuries to essentialism. No one has better described this racial straitjacketing than the existentialist psychiatrist Frantz Fanon (1925–61). Fanon speaks of his own frustrations as an Afro-Caribbean met by the essentialist gaze. He came to France from Martinique, served in the Free French Army in World War II, and graduated in medicine and psychiatry at Lyons. But his existential mobility could always be frozen by three words, 'Look, a Negro!' He is trapped in the basest category of race which denies him access to existence in history.

This predicament has resulted in the black's vulnerability to ego collapse and a sense of non-being which Fanon terms 'existential deviation'. Rage at being predetermined by others can turn against oneself in a fracture of identity that Fanon has brilliantly examined in *Black Skins, White Masks* (1952). Blacks are in peril of believing themselves at fault for the visitations of enslavement and colonization which erased them from history. Black has come to represent the very colour itself of expendable beings. Audre Lorde has put it most simply:

We have had to fight, and still do, for the very visibility which also renders us most vulnerable, our Blackness. For to survive in the mouth of this dragon we call america, we have had to learn this first and most vital lesson – that we were never meant to survive.[43]

Black is what is seen; the person is not. I am invisible in this crevice between appearance and being. Existential deviation contaminates the mind when one's native history is eliminated by slavery or, as Fanon says, by the process of colonial settlement.

The settler makes history and is conscious of making it. And because he constantly refers to the history of his mother country, he clearly indicates that he himself is the extension of that mother country. Thus the history which he writes is not the history of the country which he plunders but the history of his own nation in regard to all that she skims off, all that she violates and starves ... The immobility to which the native is condemned can only be called into question if the native decides to put an end to the history of colonization ...[44]

Fanon experienced decolonization at first-hand while serving as a psychiatrist in Algeria during its savage war of independence.

Sartre enters as a link between European and black existential philosophy. He endorsed violent decolonization in French Algeria and throughout the Third World in his preface to Fanon's book, *The Wretched of the Earth* (1961):

The rebel's weapon is proof of his humanity . . . to shoot down a European is to kill two birds with one stone, to destroy an oppressor and the man he oppresses at the same time: there remain a dead man and a free man . . .[45]

But there is more to Sartre's position than an approval of violence. He looks back to *Reflections on the Jewish Question*, essays written in 1946, which attacked France's ignoble policy of Collaboration with Nazi Germany. Sartre introduced a provocative criticism of liberal democracy at that time. He asked: Is the democrat a 'natural friend' of the Jews? No, because the democrat recognizes neither Jews, Arabs, blacks or any others 'but only man unchanged everywhere and in all periods'. Democrats end up as allies to anti-Semites in wanting 'to destroy Jews but leave only their humanity'. The democratic principle of assimilation which declares that all peoples are equal and alike is in reality a levelling of their differences to a single *essential* human nature.

Existentialists do not believe there is any such 'bottom-line' human nature but only a human *condition* which will always pose awkward differences.

There is no essential woman

Women are also susceptible to existential deviation. They too risk losing themselves in appearance. 'How do I look?' Anxiety reduces a woman's being to the judgemental gaze of men, of other rival women, and most damagingly to her own self-reflection. Veiling a woman from head to toe essentializes her as an object of desire just as nudity does at another extreme.

Such thoughts on women would not be likely without a precedent history of feminism now taken for granted. But it is in fact one tributary in a wider emancipationist movement no older than the French Revolution. We do well to recall that feminism's first stage appearance in history occurs in the 1850s, coevally with Marxism. The similarity between them is that both make us conscious of the near invisibility of a vast multitude of beings whose productive labour has long been exploited, either for economic ends, or in the case of women doubled by economic and cultural domination. This is the weight of oppression that feminists have struggled to shift by campaigning for equal rights, economic parity and social justice right up to the present day. Their success appears clearest in modern Western civilization but is limited even there.

What is the existentialist contribution to feminism?

Readers will have noted that existentialism can be freestanding, a philosophy in its own right, but that it also attaches itself as a corrective to pre-existing institutions or movements. Christianity and Marxism are two examples we have seen. Existentialism follows that pattern of independent corrective in its approach to feminism. Its first concern is with the question of women's existential deviation from authentic being. Existentialism's thought experiment on woman's being results in an unexpected conclusion. There is no essentially authentic *woman*. The question of woman's 'authentic being' involves us in fathoming the inauthenticity of that question.

Simone de Beauvoir (1908–86) achieved this first existentialist turn in feminist consciousness. Beauvoir's *The Second Sex* (1949) introduced the new and subsequently influential idea that woman has been culturally constructed as the *Other*. The category of the Other has a specific technical meaning in existentialist thought. The Other is fundamental to the formation of human subjectivity. A sense of self can only be produced by opposition to – or in Sartre's sense a negation of – that which is *not*-self. Men have taken exclusive command of selfhood and banished women to the twilight status of 'eternal Other'. Existential deviation was decisively challenged in Beauvoir's most famous utterance: 'One is not born, but rather becomes, a woman.' 'Woman' has therefore no real substance but to serve in the projection of male fantasies and fears of the Other. Women have internalized this 'myth of the Other' and even learnt to dream themselves through the dreams of men.

What does it really mean to be a 'true woman'? Beauvoir asks us to consider that its requirement is the acceptance of being an object without autonomy.

Beauvoir's analysis of how woman came to be the Other takes on biology, Freudian psychoanalysis and Marxism. All three are condemned as unacceptably determinist. Women must recover the subjecthood so far denied to them. She exhorts women to seize the opportunity of emancipation partially conceded to them to achieve complete economic and social equality. Their inner metamorphosis will follow and 'Woman' will at last exist for herself.

Beauvoir's book appeared in a period of hiatus between First Wave feminism from the 1850s to 1914 and the Second Wave in the early 1960s and '70s. Her ideas, refashioned in Betty Friedan's *The Feminine Mystique* (1963), inspired a sudden outpouring of theoretical writings. The publication of overnight classics occurred in 1970 alone: Kate Millett's *Sexual Politics*, Shulamith Firestone's *The Dialectic of Sex*, Germaine Greer's *The Female Eunuch* and several more ambitious texts.

Beauvoir's emphasis on the modern currency of feminism had taken it out of history. Or so it became for some of her less sophisticated followers. But there is still *someone other* missing from Beauvoir's category of the Other. The blind spot was identified by the African American critic bell hooks (born Gloria Watkins, 1952). Her first of many books, *Ain't I a Woman*

(1981), lodged a protest against feminism's marginalization of black women. The contentions of race and class had been effectively sidelined in the theoretical discourses of affluent white feminists. It is not enough in bell hooks's view to promote opportunities for capitalist success within reach of successfully emancipated women. She refuses the name 'feminist' so long as it remains a privileged sector of exclusion which overlooks the wider human struggle against oppression. Her provocatively uncapitalized name bears resonant witness to the anonymity of the unprivileged others. She has advanced the cause of existentialist feminism by reconnecting it to the line of pioneer African American emancipationists carried on by contemporary black liberationists. *Ain't I a Woman* quotes from one of these early black feminists, the redoubtable Sojourner Truth (1797–1883) who came up from slavery to preach the uncompromising gospel of women's rights, racial equality and economic justice: 'Look at my arm! I have ploughed, and planted, and gathered into barns, and no man could head me! And ain't I a woman?'

Two features should appear highlighted in this sketch of existentialist feminism. One is its evident inclination to ethics. The other, on which I shall end, is its intellectual vigour which does not plead for equality with men but assumes rightful parity. Existentialist women are characterized by a reluctance to identify themselves simply as 'feminist' and a preference to think and act independently of labels. This is true of the pantheon which includes Hannah Arendt, Simone Weil and Martha Nussbaum among other illustrious intellects.

Eleventh thought experiment

Is freedom the end of history?

Sartre's idea of freedom as 'lack' can be seen as a compelling creative force in history. It drives us to imagine other than lack, to negate lack, and to seek for material plenitude. Lack is in this sense a 'positive negation' of use to human beings in their constant historical struggle to overcome material scarcity. Lack has made us technologically inventive in combating scarcity. History is this competition to secure our needs in a hostile situation of scarcity.

But where does scarcity come from? Not from nature but from the competitive needs of culture. History is made in conflict for the resources that become scarce – but scarce for whom? Scarce for those deprived of them because of others who have made a value of scarcity.

Lack divides into histories of haves and have-nots. Have-nots suffer the dire negative effects of lack: they are robbed of its positive force which the haves exclusively possess.

Sartre's approach to history is to make *existential* lack consistent with freedom. It is clearly not in line with freedom to endure poverty on a mass scale. The question of history is then one of scarcity as an outright denial of being imposed by the haves on the have-nots. How can the have-nots regain the responsibility for their freedom when history has turned its back on them?

Sartre invested in Marxism as the only counterforce that could restore history to the disadvantaged. 'I consider Marxism the one philosophy of our time which we cannot go beyond,' Sartre affirmed in 1960, 'because we have not gone beyond the circumstances which engendered it.'[46] This did not mean he had abandoned existentialism but that Marxism completes existentialism and, in turn, existentialism adds a necessary human corrective to Marxism. Sartre was aware that Soviet Marxism had frozen into a monolithic tyranny guilty of crimes against humanity. It did not cause him to lose hope. He made a 'leap of faith' and looked beyond the limits of Marxism to the most far-reaching possibility of freedom that we can only dimly imagine at present:

> As soon as there will exist for everyone a margin of real free-
> dom beyond the production of life, Marxism will have lived
> out its span; a philosophy of freedom will take its place. But we
> have no means, no intellectual instrument, no concrete expe-
> rience which allows us to conceive of this freedom or of this
> philosophy.[47]

Sartre is affirming something more than a belief in humanity's future realization of freedom. He is saying that such a belief would not be possible for us if we did not already believe in freedom as a present reality. It is ultimately our choice that will transform us, or not, into beings of realized universal freedom.

Freedom is our only finality.

Twelfth thought experiment

Existentialism and the future present

Existentialists are sceptical of progress. Sartre exemplifies this scepticism. He refuses to confide in any predetermined end for humanity. His belief in an unending human project – our permanent condition of *becoming human* – leads him to deny progress. 'Existentialists do not believe in progress,' he states. 'Progress implies amelioration; but man is always the same, facing a situation which is always changing, and choice remains always a choice in the situation.'[48]

'Man is always the same'? Does this not subscribe to the essentialist belief in an unchangeable human nature? No, it does not, if we have grasped the meaning of existential fundamentals. Sartre is saying that we will always have to confront *choices* – different *unexpected* ones – but always at the same risk of self-deception.

Heidegger and Sartre issued a warning that our inclination to technological complacency is presently endangering the future. That view has become twenty-first-century common currency.

John Gray, professor of European thought at the London School of Economics, is the most lucid advocate of the view that progress is an illusion. People, he says, are 'overimpressed by recent reality' and assume, on the basis of only a couple of centuries of history, that progress is eternal . . . he argues that human nature is flawed and incorrigible and its flaws will be embodied in whatever humans make . . . institutions, therefore, do not rise above human nature: they embody it. Science, for Gray, does indeed accumulate knowledge. But that has the effect of empowering human beings to do at least as much damage as good.[49]

We have already crossed the threshold of choice foreseen by Heidegger, Sartre and other twentieth-century existentialists. Do we opt for a panicked 'doomsday scenario' or persist in our 'good faith' in progress? We have grown accustomed to gloomy forecasts like this one recently presented in the *Sunday Times Magazine*:

The figures show that economic and technological progress is loading the planet with billions more people. By keeping humans alive longer and by feeding them better, progress is continually pushing population levels. With population comes pollution. The overwhelming scientific consensus is that global warming caused by human activity is happening. According to some estimates, we will pass the point of no return within a decade. Weather systems will change, huge flooding will occur, and human civilisation if not existence will be at risk. This can be avoided if the US and China cut their carbon-dioxide emissions by 50 per cent at once. This won't happen, as they are fighting an economic war with progress as the prize. There are many other progress-created threats. Oil is one diminishing resource, and fresh water is another, even more vital one. Wars are virtually certain to be fought to gain control of these precious liquids.[50]

We are stuck on a merry-go-round of questions. Do we really need an electronic world, a superabundance of cars, cheap air travel? Can we sustain our energy-greedy consumerist civilization? Is globalization a good idea or a disaster?

The essential question is: What do we make of these questions *right now*? Do we dare hesitate to ponder if they are open-ended? Or have they already decided on our catastrophe?

The real underlying problem scripted by our questionable progress is the *future present*. There is a wide school today of scenario-builders known as futurists (they do not like to be called futurologists) who are urgently concerned with the future as a present reality. One of them, Bruce E. Tonn, has written a policy statement on the survival of 'earth-life'. His essay entitled 'Transcending Oblivion' begins with a fact:

> The earth is halfway to oblivion. Our home has reached, approximately, the midpoint of its life-sustaining existence. Created about four and a half billion years ago, the earth faces complete devastation within a similar future time horizon. This is because the sun will have reached the end of its ability to support life on earth.[51]

Four and a half billion years to oblivion may seem far too remote from our present concerns. But is it? He goes on:

> Transcending oblivion needs to be a primary guiding vision for earth-life. In other words, the goal of emigrating from earth and this solar system prior to its oblivion to inhabit other planet(s) in the universe must be set and acted upon. This formidable task may require tens of millions of years of concerted effort. With respect to the projected remaining lifespan of the sun, even if transcending oblivion requires one hundred million

years of effort, there appears to be a great deal of leeway as to how quickly this task needs to be accomplished. Halfway to oblivion, the problem appears not to be the time needed to accomplish this task as much as it is that time is of the essence to act to change current behaviour that threatens the ability to sustain and enhance the capacity for earth-life to meet this challenge. To ensure that the capacity will exist requires planning and policy horizons that far exceed those that guide human behaviour in the present time.[52]

The key point Tonn makes is that we need 'to change current behaviour'. This would most certainly involve a change of ethics with regard to 'fundamental genetic imperatives'. In his view, we must reach consensus on a programme of genetic engineering.

I have indicated that existentialists are not keen on genetic tampering. Their reasons – not necessarily religious – have to do with the unanswerable end of the human project. But suppose that our ultimate project is to sustain earth-life by genetic preparations now for future departure from this expiring planet. What then? Would existentialists not have to agree to these genetic imperatives and alter their ethical resistance to an 'end in view'?

I think not.

Yes, existentialists agree that the future is indeed present. And yes, they agree that our current unsustainable behaviour must change. And certainly, yes, existentialists agree that time is of the essence. But it is not simple linear time which threatens us with extinction.

The future is there in what we call the 'time being' which is our recognition of an unseen, fleeting present. We know ourselves to be in a force-field of time that clocks cannot adequately account for.

This existentialist intuition of time accords with our uncanny impression of being compelled by the future. We sense ourselves, so to speak, already 'futured'. Existentialism invites us to benefit from its grasp of actually experienced time. What is this benefit?

Existentialists believe there is a finite limit to our project of being. We cannot know what our end is to be. This is the limitation. It is not a negative one but a necessary corrective which permits us to question our entrapment in the illusion of progress.

Heidegger spoke of our choice 'to let Being be'. In other words, it is within our possibilities to call a halt, to retrieve ourselves from the impasse of technology as a *fait accompli*. 'Retrieved' for Heidegger signifies that which must be done again, a redeeming of history, which demands our enlightened choice. He does not intend anything like anti-science or anti-technology. We cannot retrogress to a 'better' previous state of being. An understanding of existential time would indicate that our *origin* awaits us in the future. Origin is not that from which we have progressed but what still remains to be recovered in time.

We can explore the 'genetic imperatives' with a sense of concern for our awaiting origin. Existentialists do not believe in prohibiting experiment. Their alliance to science is not one of faith but of corrective principle. It should be our scientific axiom that any knowledge which may significantly alter human *being* – to further its course of evolution, let's say, by engineering a presumed improvement – must consent to retard its implementation. The question is not what we are going to be but what we have already become by rushing into the head wind of unknown consequences.

The greatest scientific advance will be its learning that the wisest use of time is to be time-wise.

We cannot know what our fate is to be. It might be best 'to let

Being be', as Heidegger advises: to serve responsibly in the main-tenance of this planet earth, and in the end to expire calmly with it when its time is done. This is perhaps the true calling of our finite limit. We have everything to gain from being the devoted guardians of earth-life. Acceptance of limit, rather than over-reaching mastery, will prove wiser if our future is really to be extraterrestrial. We dwell in the 'time being' of either of these futures. I have called this the future present, which all existential-ists have understood as the life-world of consciousness.

Readers may note that I have given another sense to Pascal's wager on the gain or loss of infinite reward. It has to do with this *present* life. The questions we have so far encountered can be revisited in this same sense of the future present. Existentialists in this book have been seen to question the answers granted by the best-known domains of human endeavour:

Religion: *what does faith ask of me?* (This is no longer a religious question only but an existential one of being in good faith.)
Science: *has information replaced faith?*
Technology: *does it enslave or set us free?*
Philosophy: *what is the sense of being?*
Psychology: *can we account for consciousness materially?*
Ethics: *on what is moral value based?*
Aesthetics: *what is the use of the imagination?*
Politics: *is violence justified by commitment to freedom?*
History: *what are we progressing to?*

These questions do not have end-fixed answers. They are the *existential fundamentals* which accompany us on the every-day route of the future present.

No philosophy appears better suited to the future present than existentialism. There is good reason to vouch for this.

Existentialism is not a single-aimed philosophy but an adaptation to the cares of humankind which bear factual witness to a knowledge beyond the routine shortfalls of existence. What is that knowledge? It is our *unknown essence* towards which the human project of being must consciously strive but never attain. This is what existentialists believe.

Necessity makes existentialists of us all. The future is at our backs urging us on to we know not what. We can navigate better by guidance of those existentialists who have gone before, who have erred, whose adventuring in dark times has left us a map. It is a map drawn truthfully to our likeness.

Concluding interlude

Is there an existentialist geography?

> What a piercing cold I feel!
> My dead wife's comb, in our bedroom,
> Under my heel . . .
>
> *Taniguchi Buson (1715–83)*[53]

Professor Tezuka of the former Imperial University, Tokyo, visited Heidegger in his Todtnauberg mountain retreat in 1953. They exchanged reminiscences of the 1920s, when other Japanese philosophers had come to Germany to study with Husserl and Heidegger. Much of their dialogue was then spent on certain elusive Japanese aesthetic terms which do not easily translate, if at all, into concepts fathomable to the Western mind. Professor Tezuka was then led to recall Heidegger's question addressed to a Japanese colleague in 1921: 'Why do the Japanese not call back to mind the venerable beginnings of their thinking, instead of chasing ever more greedily after the latest news in European philosophy?' Tezuka lamented this sterile pursuit which still continued. How was it possible to resist the apparent technical predominance of Western thinking?

Heidegger's answer had already been given earlier in their dialogue: 'Origin always comes to meet us from the future.'[54]

There is an existentialist lesson on geography in this dialogue. Japanese thought cannot be said better or worse than European thought. Heidegger warns against surrender to such misconceived comparisons. These are the result of progress which invents a false geography of the familiar and the exotic. Heidegger asks instead, 'Where is the place of thinking?' It is not more at home in a Zen stone garden or in the pine forest of Todtnauberg. It is already in place in the difference which originally constitutes thinking. It is here, now, without geographic centre or periphery. But it also speaks in the local accent of its origin.

Heidegger's geography is an expression of time which is for us all the decisive uncertainty of being. Time is the identity of thinking which has a unique sense for each particular culture. Respect for the originality of a culture must take into account its passing in time. What has gone before in history remains for Heidegger ever-present in our duty to understand it. 'The passing of the past is something else than what has been.'[55]

This is one existentialist geography lesson. The other is that there can be no single universally valid thought. Existentialists are opposed to universalism, a benign camouflage for essentialism, posing as a 'love of humanity'. Humanity is an empty abstraction which obliterates the distinct features of language, ethnicity, culture and history. Existentialists are concerned with these specific practical situations in which human *being* recognizes itself. Being is reckoned in its given conditions of becoming. We can speak of its 'essence' only as a tendency to fulfilment which can never be realized in historical time. An example will illustrate this anti-universalist lesson.

Enrique Dussel (b.1934) is an Argentinian philosopher resident in Mexico. His existentialism has been textured by the conditions specific to Latin America. Dussel tells the story of his encounter with the masterly Jewish philosopher Emmanuel Levinas (1905–95) in the early 1970s. The young Dussel was moved to ask a question of this renowned and inspirational teacher of ethics. 'You reflect on the suffering of the Jews. Why not also consider the suffering of tens of millions of Indians and African slaves in Latin America?' Levinas looked him in the eyes and replied, 'That is for you to think about.'

Dussel took on that challenge in his lifetime's devotion to implementing a philosophy of Liberation Theology addressed to the situation of the Catholic Church in Latin America. What does the 'universal Catholic Church' mean to a Latin American peasant today? His ancestors endured centuries of colonialism and he has inherited its legacy of chronic injustice. Universality is an idea founded on the union of every practising Catholic to the Mystical Body of Christ represented on earth by the militant Church – something which the peasant experiences as local dismemberment from the benefits of a multinational corporation managed by a Vatican hierarchy. Catholicism arrived in armour-plated conquest to destroy Amerindian civilization and replace it with a so-called 'Latin' America. And yet, in spite of itself, the Church planted the seeds of liberation.

Liberation Theology takes the Eucharist seriously as a revolutionary doctrine, as an intended place-setting at the table of the hungry and dispossessed wretched of the earth. Commitment to liberation enjoins dissent from the misrepresentation of universal communion. 'I cannot take the Bread of Communion so long as I know that bread is being taken from the mouths of the poor.' Liberationists seek to restore the true sense of communion nourishment by revolutionary means if necessary.

... the theology of worldwide liberation is not easily acceptable to Europeans, who believe too passionately in their own invariable worldwide acceptance. They will not listen to the voice of the other (the barbarians, non-being if we define Being as the European way of thought), the voice of Latin America, the Arab world, or South East Asia and China ... But we know that we have taken up our stand on the farther side of the modern, oppressive, European closed system. Our minds are set upon the liberation of the poor. We point towards the world-man of the future – man who shall be eternally free.[56]

What we learn from these lessons on geography is that existentialists do not lend themselves to a population count. This book has named the existentialist celebrities, the majority of them Europeans. But there are untold numbers of existentialists labouring anonymously in Asia, Africa, the Middle East and Latin America. They are hidden by very reason of the particularities of their conditions and are most unlikely even to recognize themselves as 'existentialists'. This does not mean that anyone at all can be said an existentialist. You will know yourself one if this book has succeeded in identifing the pulse of resolute existentialist dissidence which may be characteristic of your own.

Existentialists are disinclined to speculate on the 'future of humanity'. Such thinking requires a universality which human being – and note well that I say *being* in the singular present – does not possess. It does not possess that which it presumes to benefit from – humanity, the essence which eludes it. Nevertheless, it would be inhuman not to feel any temptation to speculate.

Is it possible to anticipate what the future will look like from what already is? Science fiction excels at doing precisely that, without ever leaving the domain of advanced engineering. But I do not believe that engineering will ever us get us *physically* to the outer reaches of the galaxies. Time is the impassable barrier against bodily time-travel. Unless, maybe, we can engineer our replication by a nano-miniaturist seeding of our DNA on some other place in the universe. A memory of us will evolve elsewhere into unknowable future beings.

Perhaps we should not aspire to more than our life-world on the earth offers in such abundant splendour. This might best answer to our future. I believe the key to going further beyond is found in what is already here, in our capacity for aesthetic perfection. I think of Einstein's field equations and am awestruck by their sublime beauty. They are the numerical *haiku* of the universe. Where do these numbers come from? Where else but from the *no-thingness* of consciousness? And it responds to the phenomenal elasticity of matter. Our consciousness has theorized a worm-hole of time-travel through the matter in the universe. It could do this because it *is* the unaccountable hole in matter. It has conceived the eleven or more dimensions of string theory. This too it could do because of its scope for the inconceivable. 'To see a World in a Grain of Sand,' as William Blake famously said, is an expression of vast magnitudes enfolded in the mind.

We look to replace our fast depleting reserves of oil with alternative solar, hydrogen and nuclear energies to fuel an endlessly consumerist global economy. Our technological fix overlooks the true inexhaustible supply of energy in consciousness. If we ever do become celestial time-travellers, it will not be physically but by evolution of consciousness to a future level barely imaginable at present.

Is transport by consciousness a mere fantasy or our ultimate destiny?

What permits us to wonder is met by the radiant wonder *out there* that comes to us *here* in aesthetic revelation.

> When, with breaking heart,
> I realize
> this world is only a dream,
> the oak tree looks radiant.
>
> *Anryū Suharu (b.1923)*[57]

Such moments, when one's 'heart breaks', when all appears ephemeral as in a 'dream', can be taken as an abbreviation for all the anxiety, the utter absurdity and despair which at times swamps one's sense of being. But then the unexpected sublimity of the life-world also comes to us in time. What are these 'two times' which appear coincident in time? Are they not manifestations of another time, prophetic of what is yet-to-be? What does this time mean? To the existentialist it means that we are by obligation our own children. We, the children of time, must be raised in the existentialist belief that limitation is the only proper guideline for change. Being our own parents does not afford us the luxury of despair. 'How does one change?' The answer to the child can only tell by personal example, which may be so limited as to seem imperceptible in the worldly scheme of things. But so must our choice of being pass in children's steps towards the unknown horizon of fully human evolution. This is a belief measured by the disquiet of its own hope. And to that extent only can it be existentially valid.

> The world's darkening never reaches
> to the light of Being.[58]

References

1 Jean-Paul Sartre, *Search for a Method*, trans. Hazel E. Barnes (New York: Vintage Books, Random House, 1968), p. xxxiii

2 Albert Camus, *The Myth of Sisyphus*, (New York: Vintage Books, Alfred A. Knopf, Inc., 1991), p. 7

3 This story is found in Jean-Paul Sartre, *Existentialism and Humanism*, trans. Philip Mairet (London: Eyre Methuen, 1974)

4 Blaise Pascal, *Pensées*, trans. J. M. Cohen, (London: Penguin Books, 1961), No. 343, p. 123

5 *Pensées*, No. 84, p. 51

6 Miguel de Unamuno, *The Agony of Christianity*, trans. K. F. Reinhardt (New York: Frederick Ungar Publishing Co., 1960), p. 103

7 *The Pensées*, No. 194, p. 82

8 *The Pensées*, No. 346, p. 124

9 Camus, *The Myth of Sisyphus*, pp. 3–4

10 *The Pensées*, No. 91, p. 57

11 Ibid, No. 265, pp. 100–101

11 Camus, *The Myth of Sisyphus*, p. 95

13 Kierkegaard, *Philosophical Fragments, or a Fragment of Philosophy*, trans. D. F. Swenson and H. V. Hong (New Jersey: Princeton University Press, 1967), p. 55

14 Kierkegaard, *Works of Love*, trans. H. V. Hong and Edna H. Hong (New York: Harper and Row, 1962), p. 223

15 Nietzsche, *Twilight of the Idols*, trans. R. J. Hollingdale (London: Penguin Books, 1990), p. 21

16 Nietzsche, *Twilight of the Idols*, pp. 21–2

17 It occurs several times in Nietzsche's writings but is developed in the section, 'Of the Vision and the Riddle', in *Thus Spake Zarathustra* (London: Penguin, 1961)

18 Kierkegaard, *Repetition: An Essay in Experimental Psychology*, trans. Walter Lowrie (New York: Harper Torchbooks, 1964), p. 33

19 Sayyid Qutb, *Milestones* (New Delhi: Islamic Book Service, 1998), p. 75. Other editions of this book are titled *Signposts on the Road*.

20 Ibid, p. 12

21 Ibid, p. 158

22 Jean-Paul Sartre, *Existentialism and Humanism*, trans. Philip Mairet (London: Eyre Methuen, 1974), p. 50

23 Camus, *The Myth of Sisyphus*, p. 3

24 Ibid, p. 24

25 Ibid, p. 4

26 Ibid, p. 40

27 Ibid, p. 91

28 Paul Ricouer, *A Key to Husserl's Ideas* I, trans. Bond Harris and Jacqueline Bouchard Spurlock (Milwaukee: Marquette University Press, 1996), p. 48

29 Antoine de Saint-Exupéry, *The Little Prince*, trans. Katherine Woods (London: Reed Books, 1991), p. 73

30 Sartre, *Existentialism and Humanism*, p. 26

31 Edmund Husserl, *The Crisis of European Sciences and Transcendental Phenomenology*, trans. David Carr (Evanston: Northwestern University Press, 1970), section 41, p. 151

32 Chang Chen Chi, *The Practice of Zen* (New York: Harper & Row, 1959), p. 225

33 Husserl, *The Crisis of European Sciences*, p. 163

34 Sartre, *Search for a Method*, pp. 88 and 90

35 Husserl quoted in Hugo Ott, *Martin Heidegger: A Political Life*, trans. Allan Blunden (London: HarperCollins, 1993), p. 185

36 Martin Heidegger, 'Letter on Humanism', trans. Frank A. Capuzzi, in *Pathways*, ed. W. McNeill (Cambridge: Cambridge University Press, 1998), p. 252

37 Heidegger, *Essays in Metaphysics*, trans. Kurt F. Leidecker (New York: Philosophical Library Inc., 1960), pp. 31–2

REFERENCES   115

38 Sartre, *Being and Nothingness*, trans. Hazel E. Barnes (London: Methuen, 1957; 1966), p. 566

39 Sartre, *Being and Nothingness*, p. 572

40 Ludwig Binswanger, *Being-in-the World: Selected Papers of Ludwig Binswanger*, trans. and introduced by Jacob Needleman, (New York and London: Basic Books, 1963), p. 114

41 Binswanger, *Being-in-the-World*, p. 112

42 Ibid, p. 112

43 Audre Lorde, quoted in *Existence in Black: An Anthology of Black Existential Philosophy*, ed. Lewis R. Gordon, (New York and London: Routledge, 1997), p. xi

44 Frantz Fanon, *The Wretched of the Earth*, trans. Constance Farrington (New York: Grove Press, 1966), p. 41

45 Sartre, preface to Fanon, *The Wretched of the Earth*, pp. 18–19

46 Sartre, *Search for a Method*, pp. xxiv and 30

47 Ibid, p. 34

48 Sartre, *Existentialism and Humanism*, p. 50

49 Brian Appleyard, 'Waiting for the Lights to Go Out', *Sunday Times Magazine*, 16 October 2005, p. 35

50 Ibid, p. 37

51 Bruce E. Tonn, 'Transcending Oblivion', *Futures*, Volume 31, Numbers 3/4, April/May 1999, p. 351

52 Ibid, p. 352

53 Haiku in *A Treasury of Asian Literature*, trans. H. G. Henderson (New York: Mentor, 1958), p. 250.

54 From 'A Dialogue on Language' in *On the Way to Language*, trans. Peter D. Hertz (New York: Harper and Row, 1971), pp. 1–54

55 Ibid, p. 54

56 Enrique Dussel, *Beyond Philosophy: Ethics, History, Marxism, and Liberation Theology* (Maryland and Oxford: Rowman & Littlefield, 2003), p. 35

57 *Women Poets of Japan*, trans. Kenneth Rexroth and Ikuko Atsumi (New York: New Directions, 1977), p. 73

58 Martin Heidegger, *Poetry, Language, Thought*, trans. Albert Hofstadter (New York and London: Harper Colophon Books, 1975), p. 4

Chronology

Science, philosophy, religion and **history** are the elements of the following sequences. We will see them part and recombine like a DNA strand in the formation of existentialism.

Stage One

Science
The heliocentric theory of Nicolaus Copernicus (1473–1543) displaces humankind from the centre of the universe.

Galileo Galilei (1564–1642), astronomer, physicist and mathematician, pioneers the modern scientific worldview that physics must be separated from philosophy and true knowledge gained by experiment.

Philosophy
René Descartes (1596–1650) radicalizes Galileo's views by proposing a comprehensive doctrine of physico-mathematical reductionism to explain all material phenomena. But he also conceived of mind as an independent entity outside physics that could only be grasped by introspective reflection.

Blaise Pascal (1623–62), the first Christian existentialist, bears witness to the isolated consciousness in an infinitely material universe.

Religion
Pascal's existentialist protest veers to Jansenist puritanism itself a result of conflicting puritan fundamentalist strains in the sixteenth century

Protestant Reformation and Catholic Counter-Reformation.

The early eighteenth century is also host to pietist or 'enthusiast' revivalism in Protestant Christianity, Judaism and Islam.

Looking ahead:
Hasidism, a Jewish pietist movement, will figure in Martin Buber's existentialism.

Wahhabism, a pietist reform movement led by Muhammad bin Abdul Wahhabi (1703–87), establishes Sunni Muslim fundamentalism in Saudi Arabia. It will influence the Islamist extremism of Sayyid Qutb.

History
The Wars of Religion in France (1562–98), the Thirty Years' War (1618–48) and the English Civil War (1642–51) are at once contradictory evidence of the victories and erosions of religious belief as a free-thinking scientific Enlightenment gains momentum in the seventeenth and eighteenth centuries.

Mercantile colonialism expands across the globe in the seventeenth and eighteenth centuries.

Stage Two

Science
Isaac Newton (1642–1727), 'the greatest scientist', establishes systematic physics on the mathematical principles of mechanics and gravitation.

Mechanization descends from cosmology to systematize everyday productive life in steam-age industrial mechanics and the 'dismal science' of political economy instituted by Adam Smith (1723–90) and the British school.

Philosophy
Galileo and Descartes' theories of knowledge influence the empiricism of John Locke (1632–1704) which opens a new chapter on the psychology of conscious perception.

David Hume (1711–76) develops a more radical psychology of empiricist scepticism in his theory of the natural constraints on knowledge which parallels Newtonian mechanics.

Immanuel Kant (1724–1804) divorces self-consciousness from its apparent source of knowledge in the perception of objects. This is Kant's 'Copernican revolution' in philosophy.

G. W. F. Hegel (1770–1831) swept away these boundaries on consciousness to arrive at an all-comprehensive system of history whose end is Absolute Reason.

The earlier empirical sceptics figure indirectly in Søren Kierkegaard's (1813–55) existentialist collision with Hegel's hyper-idealist system of reason.

Karl Marx (1818–83) too sets out from Hegel's idealism on his leftist road to atheistic Historical Materialism. But whereas Marx proceeds by anchoring his materialism to the mechanics of productive labour and the economic theories of capitalism, Kierkegaard's reckoning has to do with faith in a Christianity subverted by a mechanically rational world.

Both thinkers inherit a critical philosophical legacy which permits them to unmask 'false consciousness' – the capitalist one which for Marx disguises the reality of labour and the one of Christendom's bad faith which disguises the reality of Christianity for Kierkegaard.

Religion
The acceleration of modernity in the eighteenth and nineteenth centuries sharpens the conflict between secularism and the fundamentalist currents. This can be seen in late eighteenth-century Wesleyan Methodism, other trends of evangelical revivalism and the Spiritualism craze in mid-nineteenth century America which laps over to Europe.

Looking ahead:
These evangelical trends are not simply anti-rationalist throwbacks but often the kin of social and labour reform movements as alternatives to capitalist technological modernity. The profound longing for a nonconformist spiritual imperative will remain a catalyst of Christian and other religious varieties of existentialism in the twentieth century.

History

The nineteenth century Age of Empires opens with the Industrial Revolution in the 1750s, the American Revolution (1775–83), the French Revolution (1789–99) and the Napoleonic era (1799–1815). This is also the age of Wars of National Liberation in nineteenth-century Europe and Latin America.

Stage Three

Science

Charles Darwin (1809–82) propounds a theory of evolution with long-term consequences for biology and the advancement of genetics.

Clinical psychiatry, experimental psychology and psychoanalysis appear in the late nineteenth century with Darwinist alliances to the human sciences of anthropology and sociology further developed in the twentieth century.

Philosophy

Friedrich Nietzsche (1844–1900) is the existentialist 'announcing angel' of Western civilization in moral decadence and its gathering shadows of totalitarianism. Nietzsche's forecast of an ambiguous 'super-being' might suggest Nazism's 'blond beast' but is more likely to mean 'striving to overcome oneself'. The same applies to the Islamic word *jihad* which is usually translated simply as 'holy war' but should have the preferred meaning of 'the strife in overcoming one's personal faults'.

Nietzsche and Marx can be compared in their response to the Darwinism of the industrial age of imperialism. Whereas Nietzsche resists with supreme irony the notion of a 'survival of the fittest', Marx fastens economics onto evolutionary theory in his one 'iron law' of progress towards socialist revolution.

Nietzsche is in this sense a first 'postmodern' antagonist of all grand ideas that aspire to metaphysical certitude and inevitability.

Religion

Another legacy of Hegelianism is its historicist strand which combining archaeology with the influence of evolutionary theory will lead to a scientific 'Higher Criticism' of the Bible's authentic sources and the 'search for the historical Jesus' in the academic circles of Protestant northern Europe.

But there are also reform counter-movements to modern secularism and Western colonialism.

The pan-Islamic reform led by Jamal al-Din al-Afghani (1838–97) seeks to reconcile Islam with modernity and nationalism – another contributing link to Sayyid Qutb's revolutionary Islamism.

The Meiji Restoration (1868) in Japan adopts a state doctrine of neo-Shintoism and spurs a revival of populist Buddhist sects which will later be imported to the West.

Cardinal John Henry Newman (1801–90) offers a model of established religion's adaptation to modernity. He can be seen linked to Kierkegaard's existential Christianity – which harks back to Lutheran reform – and the medieval theology of Thomas Aquinas (c. 1225–74). The special virtue of Thomism is its insistence that there should not be a conflict between faith and reason, a flexibility of doctrine which Kierkegaard's fideism lacks. Newman's progress in this line is to affirm a developmental Christian doctrine which reconciles it to Darwinism and other scientific advances.

Newman's proto-modernist Christianity looks ahead to the evolutionary theories of the Jesuit palaeontologist Pierre Teilhard de Chardin (1881–1955) whose genial idea of a human 'noosphere' – the evolution of a consciousness *instinct* – urges us to take decisive ecological responsibility for the whole planetary biosphere.

History
The Wars of National Liberation in nineteenth-century Europe and Latin America are characteristic of Romantic self-determination and emancipation. These wars in the so-called 'Third World' sector of Latin America also herald the anti-colonial movements in the Islamic world, in Japan and elsewhere which anticipate fully fledged decolonization in the twentieth century.

Stage Four

Science

Can mathematics be reduced to the psychological workings of the mind or is it reducible only to the ineluctable truths of logic? This inner circle debate between 'psychologism' and 'logicism' at the end of the nineteenth century introduced Edmund Husserl (1859–1938) to philosophy. Initially a logicist, but also shaped by the new introspectionist school of experimental psychology, Husserl turned to the study of consciousness itself which he named phenomenology.

The question of the 'truth of numbers' would indeed prove crucial to mathematical physics in its advance beyond Galileo and Newton. The turning-point came with Quantum Theory in 1900, followed fast by Einstein's Relativity theories in 1905 and 1916, the establishment of atomic theory and particle physics in 1911 and the oddity of Heisenberg's quantum Uncertainty Principle in 1927.

Philosophy

Husserl's investigations of consciousness are informed by these 'crisis worlds' of mathematics and psychology. Husserl begins his exercises in psychology by skipping back to Cartesian introspection and the empiricist accounts of consciousness in Locke, Hume and Kant to arrive at his own findings.

The genealogy of modern existentialism then branches out from Husserlian phenomenology to what might seem incompatible varieties.

The first to appear is Karl Jaspers (1883–1969) who experiments briefly with phenomenology in psychiatry but develops his own 'existence philosophy'.

We can trace Ludwig Binswanger (1881–1966) to Jasper's pioneer psychiatric work, but the existential analysis pursued by Binswanger sticks firmly to Husserl, Heidegger and the discoveries of Freudian psychoanalysis.

Martin Heidegger (1889–1976) adapted Husserlian phenomenology to a different pitch of 'existential analysis' which addresses Being in the everyday disguise of being-in-the-world.

Heidegger returns to Hegel, Kierkegaard and Nietzsche, in contrast to Husserl's disinterest in them, and also weaves the pre-Socratics, medieval theology and other strands of Western and Eastern philosophy into his rethinking of Being.

Jean-Paul Sartre (1905–80) uses phenomenology differently again to probe the nothingness of consciousness and the existential situations of freedom. Sartre passed from an early interest in neo-Kantianism to an appreciation of Hegel and especially Marx in his later philosophy. Marxism and Third World liberationism link Sartre to the psychiatrist and black militant Frantz Fanon (1925–61) and the African American existentialists. Fanon's practice of liberation psychiatry in Algeria can be linked to Binswanger's *Daseinsanalyse* method and Sartre's 'existential psychoanalysis' – both relevant to the psycho-social conditions of colonized peoples.

History

The twentieth century scene is set by the mechanized carnage of 'total war' and the final contest between Europe's imperial dynasties in World War I (1914–18). The geo-political consequences of the Great War are well known. Totalitarianism arose from its ashes in various competitive forms: Fascism in Italy (1922–45), Nazism in Germany (1933–45) and the Russian Revolution (1917) which descended to the tyranny of Stalinism (1929–53). These regimes promoted aggression to an unprecedented degree of genocide before and during World War II (1939–45). Many millions perished in the Nazi and Stalinist holocausts – a number further escalated by the arrival of Maoism in China (1949–76).

The European counter-fascist Resistance for all its flaws and limits was the human face of combat – a case less easily made for the Allied Forces napalming of German and Japanese civilians and the A-bombing of Japanese cities. Those comfortable with justifying Allied retaliation must also accept the consequent Cold War superpower deadlock in nuclear Mutually Assured Destruction (MAD). The new geo-political game plans of the Cold War era (1947–90) often camouflage the mass independence struggles of that time. Liberation movements occurred in India (1947), Africa in the 1950s, Cuba (1959), Algeria (1954–62), Vietnam (1946–76) and elsewhere.

The existentialists so far named in Stage Four were either affected by or directly enmeshed in the historical catastrophes of the twentieth century.

Edmund Husserl suffered the ignominy of being declared a Jewish 'non-person' by Nazi thugs.

Karl Jaspers in the Nazi period survived in constant dread of arrest because of his views and Jewish wife.

Martin Heidegger gave brief allegiance to Hitler and remained thereafter tarnished by Nazism.

Jean-Paul Sartre, Simone de Beauvoir and Albert Camus were either active or professed solidarity with the French Resistance.

Religion
It is instructive to consider the effects of twentieth century history on some of the religious existentialists.

Nikolai Berdyaev (1874–1948) initially attracted to Marxism was expelled from the Soviet Union in 1922 and settled in Paris. He turned to a form of messianic Russian Orthodoxy – as interpreted by the novelist Fyodor Dostoevsky (1821–81) – in which 'The Christ' is a prefigurement of future liberated humankind.

Martin Buber (1878–1965) was forbidden to teach by the Nazi secret police and emigrated in 1938 to Palestine. Buber's existentialism is an interesting compound of Hasidic pietism, rabbinic lore, Kiergekaardian Christian mysticism and Chung Tzu's Taoism – but it was Nietzsche's influence which turned him to campaign for Zionism in 1901. Buber understood Zionism as essentially a spiritual and collective renewal of Jewry and was foresighted in advocating the then and still unpopular cause of a binational Jewish-Arab state in Palestine.

Paul Tillich (1886–1965), the theologian of existential Lutheranism, served as military chaplain in World War I. The experience convinced him that Western civilization was in chaos and nearing its end. He responded by joining a Christian Socialist movement which adhered to a new social gospel of impending historical transformation. His early criticism of Nazism barred him from German universities and in 1933 he emigrated to America where he subsequently abandoned a socialist programme in favour of a more conservative 'theology of culture'.

Jacques Maritain (1882–1973), a French Protestant by origin, converted to Catholicism in 1906. After studying biology he devoted himself to the study of Thomas Aquinas. He reconstructed Thomism as a modern 'Existentialist Intellectualism'. Maritain was fortunate to be a visiting university professor in America when France fell to German occupation – especially so because he too like Jaspers had a Jewish wife.

Gabriel Marcel (1889–1973), often said the first French existentialist, was also an immensely gifted musician and dramatist. He served with the French Red Cross in World War I. By origin agnostic – with a lapsed Catholic father and nonreligious Jewish stepmother – he converted to Catholicism in 1929 by spiritual disposition but never spoke as its theological apologist. He responded to the predicament of the French people under German occupation by delving into the religious themes of exile, captivity, fidelity and hope.

Simone Weil (1909–43), of French Jewish origin, was a fiercely independent and mystical being attracted to extreme sacrificial risks of her life. She abandoned teaching to become a convert of leftwing syndicalism and a factory worker. Weil joined an Anarchist combat unit in the Spanish Civil War, the French Resistance in 1942 and journeyed to England to participate in the Free French Forces. She espoused a mystical Catholic existentialism but never consented to baptism. Her death in 1943, ruled a suicide by the coroner, was apparently due to voluntary starvation undertaken in solidarity with the suffering of the occupied French nation.

Sayyid Qutb (1906–66), the martyr ideologue of revolutionary Islamism, has been named an example of existentialism 'gone wrong'. We can disapprove of his violent 'social gospel' but still attend to the conditions which provoked him to it. Qutb voices the post-colonial ideals of the Muslim Brotherhood, founded in 1922, which underwent the frustrations and defeats of pan-Arab nationalism. His embitterment parallels the fate of the early twentieth-century Salafiyyah reform movement in the Middle East. Its failure to reconcile Islam with modernist secularism led to its own opposite and present aggressively fundamentalist transformation.

Existentialists cannot always be said to practise a perfectly exemplary virtue. They have often been tempted to seize on what appears to be the 'revolutionary initiative' which brought Sartre and others to the left or a fall to the right in Heidegger's case.

Enrique Dussel (b. 1934) advocates a Christian existentialism allied to the liberation movements of the 1960s and '70s geo-politically specific to the Third World conditions of Latin America and its grotesque dictatorships endorsed by corporate America. Dussel's programme of Liberation Theology can be seen situated between the 'demytholo-gized Christianity' of the 1950s – a Western secularist gentrification of Christianity which sheds its sacramental and revolutionary 'social gospel' – and Vatican Council II (1962–65) which promoted a Liberation Theology that briefly renewed but also disappointed hopes in the universalism of a nonconformist message relevant to the world's poor.

Dussel's criticism of a Eurocentric colonialist Christianity encourages existentialism to double back on itself and ask, 'Where is your social gospel?' And it does so precisely amid the conditions of the Cold War which mesmerized the attention of the affluent West on its own overrid-ing capitalist survival. Liberation Theology was and remains a call to take undistracted heed of earth-life in its wholeness. Doubling back on existentialism also allows us to reconsider it as a whole – for instance, to uncover the ecological and Marxist undercurrents of Heidegger's thought on Being.

Stage Five

Looking ahead: A programme for twenty-first-century existentialism

Science and the age of consciousness
We call it by many names. Postmodernity, the end of history, the post-industrial age, globalization and the age of information technology are some of them. It is in essence a by-product era of previous scientific and technological advances characterized by the three interlocking elements of *coding*, *miniaturization* and *virtual simulations of reality*.

These features are exemplified by molecular biology's discovery of DNA (1953) and the human genome project which refers to the sum total of genetic information microscopically encoded in our chromosomal make-up.

So too is true for the Big Bang Theory (1965) issued from quantum ideas and research into the infinitely tiny sub-atomic realm which has culminated – or come to grief – in superstring theory's multi-universe concealed in eleven dimensions.

Alan Turing's mathematically defined 'universal machine' in 1936 did more than open the path to computers – it initiated experimental research into the virtual simulation of human consciousness by artificially intelligent robotic beings. Computerology speedily progressed to the internet (1969) and our immersion in a present digital environment.

In each of these progressions something inconceivably colossal – the bio-molecular domain of genes, the cosmos, the mega-network of information in the ether – is at once invisible and yet functionally in reach of miniaturized coding programmes.

The startling evidence is that human consciousness has become dissociated from the technological manifestations of its own doing which are now in the process of transforming it.

We are being re-equipped from the outside by an alternate consciousness liberated from us by our investment in technological simulation.

It is this same de-centred human being who longs for space travel into the far beyond of this earth.

Is there a new existentialism that can cope with this apparently irreversible transformation of consciousness?

History
The end of the Cold War era has brought us to another sort of history whose main channel for all eventualities is the media. This too has been called an extension of virtual reality technology in which events are instantaneously processed as global information and equally speedily become obsolete and replaced. We end up with an endlessly escalating and yet repetitive information spectacle which feeds on anxiety but promotes apathy.

The witch-doctors of postmodernity have pronounced ad nauseam on this 'simulated reality' – and their pessimism is not without foundation. A symptom rather than the illness has been diagnosed.

How might a new generation of existentialists respond to this problem of an ever-present media 'instant history'?

We cannot risk proceeding with history as we have so far conceived of it – a chronology of significant human events. It has not yet been properly acknowledged that such a history of 'human eventfulness' must be reconceived and overcome by a history of the planetary life-world. Our real history is that of an endangering and consequently endangered species. Alas, perhaps only a global catastrophe will bring us to our senses, and then to acknowledge our latecomer and parasitic role in real history.

The information age has rendered us sightless in face of a comprehensive reality. Ecology took its first steps in 1962 and James Lovelock put forward his Gaia Hypothesis in 1979. These have partially restored us to sight of that which is indeed encompassingly huge but not more than the horizon of our unique life-world.

Religion
Religion has not exposed its unfeasibility but rather the unsustainability of present human misbehaviour.

Every religion is a potential mine of spiritual technologies available to enrich consciousness evolution if, and only, if we can liberate the spiritual imperative itself from the abuses of human ignorance.

The case is made for atheism as a benign humanist alternative to the crimes of religion. It must never be forgotten that atheism has given us the dire 'social gospels' of totalitarianism implemented by Mussolini, Hitler, Stalin and Mao with appalling genocidal results far worse than religions ever wrought.

There is an inkling 'through a glass darkly' that we have come to the end of divisive religions without yet seeing how their incompatibilities might be superseded by the existential fundamentals of a 'real history' spirituality liberated from institutional boundaries.

Traces of a route are already evident in the journeys of existentialists of the past. But a new existentialism has not yet come to double back enough on itself to retrieve from the past what is of urgent and present redemptive use for the future.

Philosophy

What do we understand by 'human improvement'? Is it a materially engineered improvement that we favour? Genetic interventions not only offer us medical advantages in the short-term future but the possibility of redesigning the human species. We lack a philosophy with sufficient ethical perspective to inform our decisions now on the future benefits or catastrophes of evolution by genetic programme management.

There is no 'philosophy' at present which answers to the case for consciousness evolution. Nor can there be one which is not able to accommodate a unitary combination of science, religion and philosophy on the ground of real life-world history.

This combinative fifth stage of existentialism awaits materialization in the future present of **transmodernity**, a watchword rumoured by Enrique Dussel, and a work in progress by like-minded thinkers proceeding in cooperation.

Index